365 DAILY MEDITATIONS WITH POPE FRANCIS

United States Conference of Catholic Bishops
Washington, DC

First printing, November 2015

ISBN 978-1-60137-475-2

Contents

NEW YEAR'S ADVICE FROM THE HOLY FATHER

Take care of your spiritual life, your relationship with God, because this is the backbone of all that we do and all that we are.

For today, make a New Year's resolution to set aside time each day to strengthen your relationship with God through prayer. In honor of the World Day of Peace, pray for an end to violence in our world and for a peaceful beginning to the New Year.

OPEN THE DOOR FOR JESUS

Ask yourselves this question: How often is Jesus inside and knocking at the door to be let out, to come out? And we do not let him out because of our own need for security, because so often we are locked into ephemeral structures that serve solely to make us slaves and not free children of God.

For today, spend some quiet time listening for Jesus and reflecting on how he is calling you to do good things in the world.

FAITH IS A GUIDING LIGHT

Faith is not a light which scatters all our darkness, but a lamp which guides our steps in the night and suffices for the journey. To those who suffer, God does not provide arguments which explain everything; rather, his response is that of an accompanying presence, a history of goodness which touches every story of suffering and opens up a ray of light.

For today, be a light in the world. Consider visiting a senior citizen who lives alone or helping out at a retirement center. Reach out to a friend in need.

POISONOUS GOSSIP

Gossip can also kill, because it kills the reputation of the person! It is so terrible to gossip! At first it may seem like a nice thing, even amusing, like enjoying a candy. But in the end, it fills the heart with bitterness, and even poisons us.

For today, vow to avoid gossip. Refuse to listen to or spread rumors about others.

A JOYFUL CHRISTIAN

J oy cannot be held at heel: it must be let go. Joy is a pilgrim virtue. It is a gift that walks, walks on the path of life, that walks with Jesus: preaching, proclaiming Jesus, proclaiming joy, lengthens and widens that path.

For today, share your joy in life by offering a kind word and a smile to those you encounter. Let your joy show in your face and in your actions, in everything you do this day.

SAY YES TO GOD

The Living God sets us free! Let us say "yes" to love and not selfishness. Let us say "yes" to life and not death. Let us say "yes" to freedom and not enslavement to the many idols of our time. In a word, let us say "yes" to the God who is love, life and freedom, and who never disappoints.

For today, reflect on the ways in which you can reject selfishness and idols. What can you say no to today in order to say yes to God?

A WELCOMING PLACE

May the Church be a place of God's mercy and hope, where all feel welcomed, loved, forgiven and encouraged to live according to the good life of the Gospel. And to make others feel welcomed, loved, forgiven and encouraged, the Church must be with doors wide open so that all may enter. And we must go out through these doors and proclaim the Gospel.

For today, consider the ways in which you can help make the Church a welcoming place of God's mercy and hope. Seek someone to whom you can provide encouragement; invite him or her to attend Mass or a church gathering with you.

LIVING IN LOVE

Christian love always possesses one quality: concreteness. Christian love is concrete. Jesus himself, when he speaks of love, tells us concrete things: feed the hungry, visit the sick.

For today, consider one concrete way you can show someone Christian love. Call an elderly relative or acquaintance on the telephone, or—if possible—arrange to take him or her a meal. Prepare enough for two so that you can stay and enjoy the meal with that person.

WHAT DO I DO FOR GOD?

If I abide in Jesus, if I abide in the Lord, if I abide in love, what do I do for God—not what do I think or what do I say—and what do I do for others? . . . The first criteria is to love with deeds, not with words. . . . The wind carries away our words: today they are here and tomorrow they are gone.

For today, love someone with a kind deed instead of just your words. Plan a special surprise for your spouse or a family member who isn't expecting it.

10

PEOPLE OF HOPE

There are many Christians with a hope too watered down, not strong: a faint hope. . . . If we Christians believe [in] confessing the faith, and safeguarding it, taking custody of the faith, and, entrusting ourselves to God, to the Lord, we shall be Christian victors—and this is the victory that has overcome the world: our faith.

For today, confess your faith in God through prayer. Is something troubling you? Are you struggling with a personal challenge or obstacle? Turn it over to God, and have faith he will help you find the answer or give you strength to deal with it. Be a strong, hopeful Christian.

GO OUT AND SERVE

W e who are Christians, members of God's family, are called to go out to the needy and to serve them.

For today, seek an opportunity to serve someone who needs a helping hand in your community. Sign up to volunteer at a soup kitchen, at a food pantry, or through a committee at your church.

FORGIVENESS

Take care of the wounds of the heart with the oil of forgiveness, forgiving the people who have injured us and treating the injuries that we have inflicted on others.

For today, pray for someone who has personally hurt you in some way. Ask God to help you find forgiveness within your heart for that person.

GOD PREPARES US

God in his love prepares the way, and he prepares our lives for each of us. . . . He does not make us Christians through spontaneous generation. He prepares our path, he prepares our lives over time.

For today, think of two ways God has prepared the way for you over time to lead a Christian life. How might he continue to prepare your path in the future?

14

BE WATCHFUL

Eliminate the rancor that leads us to vengeance, and the laziness that leads us to existential euthanasia, the finger-pointing that leads to arrogance, and the continual complaining that leads us to desperation.

For today, write down three good things that have happened to you this week. When you feel tempted to complain today or any day this week, pull out the list, and send up a quick prayer of gratitude.

RACISM IS EVIL

M any people who are forced into emigration suffer and often die tragically; many of their rights are violated, they are obliged to separate from their families and, unfortunately, continue to be subjected to racist attitudes and xenophobia. . . . A change of attitude toward migrants and refugees is needed on the part of everyone, moving away from attitudes of defensiveness and fear, indifference and marginalization.

For today, on the birthday of Dr. Martin Luther King Jr., resolve to put all prejudices aside, and remember that all of us are brothers and sisters in our Father's eyes. Take a few minutes to read about Dr. King's accomplishments today, if you have the opportunity to do so.

January 16

BE SILENT TODAY

There is so much noise in the world! May we learn to be silent in our hearts and before God.

For today, turn off your cell phone, computer, and television for a short time, and rest in silence with God. Reflect, pray, and listen to God's message for you.

AVOID ENVY

Eliminate envy, concupiscence, hatred and the negative feelings that devour our inner peace and turn us into ruined and destructive people.

For today, consider a person for whom you have negative feelings. Perhaps that person has hurt your feelings, or you just don't care for some aspect of his or her personality. List one or two positive things about that person, and resolve to recognize something positive in every person you encounter today.

PRAY THROUGHOUT THE DAY

A sk yourselves: "How much space do I give to the Lord? Do I stop to talk with Him?" Ever since we were children, our parents have taught us to start and end the day with a prayer, to teach us to feel that the friendship and the love of God accompanies us. Let us remember the Lord more in our daily life!

For today, try to recognize the presence of God beside you at different times as you move throughout the day, and say a simple prayer of thanks for his friendship and guidance.

FREEDOM FROM A HARDENED HEART

Let us ask the Lord for the grace to have a docile heart: that He save us from the slavery of a hardened heart . . . [and] lead us to that beautiful freedom of perfect love, the freedom of the children of God, which the Holy Spirit alone can give.

For today, ask, Against whom or what have I hardened my heart? Then ask God to heal you and grant you a docile heart so that you can be free to spread God's message of love and hope to others.

A PERSONAL RELATIONSHIP WITH GOD

The Lord's relationship with his people . . . is a personal relationship, always. It is a person to person relationship. He is the Lord, and the people have a name. Persons have a name. It is not a dialogue between the Almighty and the masses. . . . Persons are organized as a people, and the dialogue is with the people; and in a people, each person has a place.

For today, ask, How is my relationship with God? What can I do to strengthen that relationship and make it more personal?

BE DOCILE TO GOD'S WORD

L et us ask for the grace of docility to God's word, to this word that is living and active, that discerns the thoughts and intentions of the heart.

For today, pray for the courage to accept the path on which the Holy Spirit is leading you in your heart.

RESPECT FOR HUMAN LIFE

The common home of all men and women must continue to rise on the foundations of a right understanding of universal fraternity and respect for the sacredness of every human life, of every man and every woman, the poor, the elderly, children, the infirm, the unborn, the unemployed, the abandoned, those considered disposable.

For today, say a prayer of thanksgiving for the wonderful gift of human life and all life. Recall how all life has been created by our loving God and reflects his majesty and wonder. Think about the ways in which you and the people around you are an image of God. Tell the Lord all the things you are grateful for—he loves gratitude.

A GOOD QUESTION

The prayer of praise is a Christian prayer for all of us. . . . We praise: you are great. "Glory be to the Father, and to the Son, and to the Holy Spirit. . . ." We say this with all our heart. It is also an act of justice, for he is great, he is our God. Let us think about a good question we can ask ourselves today: How is my prayer of praise?

For today, praise God with your heart, not just with your lips. Praise him joyously. Make an effort to leave behind your composure a little to sing next time you're at Mass.

GOD'S GIFT OF COMMUNICATION

Media can help us to feel closer to one another, creating a sense of the unity of the human family which can in turn inspire solidarity and serious efforts to ensure a more dignified life for all. Good communication helps us to grow closer, to know one another better, and ultimately, to grow in unity. The walls which divide us can be broken down only if we are prepared to listen and learn from one another.

For today, on the Memorial of St. Francis de Sales, resolve to use social media or other forms of communication as a means to listen and learn from others and to increase your understanding of the world and all of God's people.

CAREFUL DECISION MAKING

I am always wary of decisions made hastily. I am always wary of the first decision, that is, the first thing that comes to my mind if I have to make a decision. This is usually the wrong thing. I have to wait and assess, looking deep into myself, taking the necessary time.

For today, reflect on the decisions you make every day. Do you make them carefully or impulsively? Do you have an important decision to make? Look deep inside your heart for the answer, and ask God to guide you.

SHARE YOUR FAITH

E very Christian community must be a welcoming home for those searching for God, for those searching for a brother or sister to listen to them.

For today, share your Christian faith through kind words and small gestures, or by asking questions and showing a sincere interest in the lives of others.

IN REMEMBRANCE

A uschwitz cries out with the pain of immense suffering and pleads for a future of respect, peace and encounter among peoples.

For today, pray for tolerance and respect among all people, races, religions, and countries.

28

STAND FOR PEACE

Grant us the grace to be ashamed of what we men have done, to be ashamed of this massive idolatry, of having despised and destroyed our own flesh which you formed from the earth, to which you gave life with your own breath of life. Never again, Lord, never again!

For today, remember all those who have suffered the evils of intolerance, racism, terrorism, and all forms of violence. Vow to be a messenger of peace and to promote tolerance in your family, your workplace, and your community.

TAKE A CHANCE ON GOD

If up till now you have kept [the risen Jesus] at a distance, step forward. He will receive you with open arms.

For today, reflect on the ways in which following Jesus is difficult for you. Ask him to help you put aside your fear and trust in him.

ALL CHRISTIAN, ALL THE TIME

We are not Christian "part-time," only at certain moments, in certain circumstances, in certain decisions; no one can be Christian in this way—we are Christian all the time! Totally!

For today, think about the ways in which being a Christian is sometimes difficult. How can you overcome those difficulties to become a full-time Christian?

MONEY CAN ENSLAVE

I f we are too attached to riches, we are not free. We are slaves.

For today, reflect on how much value you place on material things. Do you often work extra hours to afford nice things—sacrificing time with your family or friends, or even your own freedom?

February 1

CELEBRATE DIVERSITY

I nequality is the root of social evil.

For today, pray for racial equality as we remember and honor the contributions of African Americans during Black History Month in the United States. If possible, read a news article or personal interest story about the contributions of African Americans in your community.

PRAY FOR THOSE WHO ARE CALLED

A nd in the consecrated life we live the encounter between the young and the old, between observation and prophecy. Let's not see these as two opposing realities! Let us rather allow the Holy Spirit to animate both of them, and a sign of this is joy: the joy of observing, of walking within a rule of life; the joy of being led by the Spirit, never unyielding, never closed, always open to the voice of God that speaks, that opens, that leads us and invites us to go toward the horizon.

For today, on the Feast of the Presentation of the Lord and World Day for Consecrated Life, pray for those who are called to religious orders. If your church celebrates Candlemas, attend and participate. How can you also reflect the light of Jesus in the world?

OUR PATIENT FATHER

God is patient with us because he loves us, and those who love are able to understand, to hope, to inspire confidence; they do not give up, they do not burn bridges, they are able to forgive.

For today, tell someone you know who is struggling that you have confidence in—and will stand by—him or her during this time, just as God stands by us when we need him. If you have children, reassure them that you love them and have hope for their future.

SEEK HUMILITY

The world tells us to seek success, power and money; God tells us to seek humility, service and love.

For today, consider some ways you might devote your time, talents, and energy outside of your career or place of employment to provide a service in your community. Seek humility, not accolades, for your service.

GOD WAITS FOR US

Let us remember this in our lives as Christians: God always waits for us, even when we have left him behind! He is never far from us, and if we return to him, he is ready to embrace us.

For today, ask, Have I left God behind? Have I gotten so busy with my life that I forget to pray, to thank God for the gift of each new day? Return to him and spend some quiet time today in contemplation.

February 6

WHAT IS
YOUR LEGACY?

Grant us these three graces: to ask for the grace to die at home, within the Church; to ask for the grace to die with hope; and to ask for the grace to leave behind a beautiful legacy, a human legacy, a legacy made from the witness of our Christian life.

For today, reflect on what you've accomplished so far in your life. Do you have regrets? Will you be remembered for your career achievements and material gains or for your good works and commitment to the service of others? How would you rather be remembered?

THE ART OF GOD'S PLAN

The testimony of faith comes in very many forms, just as in a great fresco, there is a variety of colors and shades, yet they are all important, even those which do not stand out. In God's great plan, every detail is important, even yours, even my humble little witness, even the hidden witness of those who live their faith with simplicity in everyday family relationships, work relationships, friendships.

For today, recognize that you, your neighbor, your coworkers, and everyone you meet today are an important part of God's plan. Nobody is more or less important in God's eyes.

8

PRAY FOR AN END TO ALL SLAVERY

But slavery is a reality woven into the social fabric today, and for a long time! Slave labor, human trafficking, the trade of children . . . it's a tragedy! Let's not close our eyes to this! Slavery, today, is a reality, the exploitation of people.

For today, pray for the safe return or release of all people, especially children, who are or who have been victims of slavery. Pray for an end to the exploitation of people.

GENEROUS ACTS

Christians knows how to give. Their lives are filled with generous acts—often hidden—toward their neighbor.

For today, anonymously do something special for your neighbor or an acquaintance you don't know well. Don't expect anything in return, and don't take credit. Make it a gift from the heart.

PUT CHRIST AT THE CENTER

We cannot be Christians part-time. If Christ is at the center of our lives, he is present in all that we do.

For today, reflect on how Christ is—or can be—at the center of your life. Do you attend Mass regularly? Pray daily? Do you talk about God with your children or the other young people in your life and teach them to pray?

PRAY ON THE WORLD DAY OF THE SICK

I entrust this World Day of the Sick to the maternal protection of Mary, who conceived and gave birth to Wisdom incarnate: Jesus Christ, our Lord.

For today, on the feast day of Our Lady of Lourdes, pray for all those who are sick, that they may find peace and consolation through their faith.

WHAT IS GOD'S PLAN FOR YOU?

Every time we give in to selfishness and say "No" to God, we spoil his loving plan for us.

For today, turn toward God for answers when facing a tough decision. Does he want you to do something difficult? Don't give in to selfishness. Trust God to help you make the right choice.

PUT ASIDE PRIDE

Humility saves man: pride makes him lose his way.

For today, resolve to be more humbler about your achievements; avoid the temptation to brag. Remember that the talents and gifts that enable you to achieve important things are not of your own making; they are gifts from God. Thank him.

14

THE GIFT OF OTHER PEOPLE

It is important to keep alive the awareness that the other person is a gift from God—and for the gifts of God we say thank you!

For today, thank the special people in your life for everything they do—and remember to thank God, too, for the gift of those special people!

PRACTICE COURTESY AT HOME

Yes, courtesy kindles love. And today in our families, in our world, which is frequently violent and arrogant, there is so much need for courtesy. And this can begin at home.

For today, remember to practice courtesy and good manners in your home and workplace, even in the face of arrogance. Plan some time, if you have children or grandchildren, to discuss the importance of displaying courtesy and kindness toward others at school and at home.

PRAY THE OUR FATHER OR ROSARY

Praying the Our Father together, around the table, is not something extraordinary: it's easy. And praying the Rosary together, as a family, is very beautiful and a source of great strength!

For today, pray together with members of your family, if possible. Pray for families who are struggling with poverty, addiction, or illness. Consider praying the Our Father before dinner and the Rosary before bedtime.

CHARITY BRINGS HAPPINESS

How marvelous it would be if, at the end of the day, each of us could say: today I have performed an act of charity toward others!

For today, reflect on how much happier you feel after you have done something unexpected for someone who needs help. What can you do for someone today that will increase both your happiness and theirs?

REACH OUT

Instead of being just a church that welcomes and receives by keeping the doors open, let us try also to be a church that finds new roads, that is able to step outside itself and go to those who do not attend Mass, to those who have quit or are indifferent.

For today, gently encourage a friend or family member who has left the Church or grown indifferent to consider attending Mass with you or to simply join you in discussion or prayer.

PRAY FOR THE WORLD

L et us always pray for one another. Let us pray for the whole world, that there may be a great spirit of fraternity.

For today, after you have finished praying for those you know and for those closest to you, pray for peace and good will among all people of the world.

PRAY FOR THOSE WHO ARE JEALOUS OF OTHERS

Today . . . let us pray for our Christian communities, that the seed of jealousy not be sown among us; that envy have no place in our hearts, and in the hearts of our communities. In this way, we can go forward joyously praising the Lord.

For today, remember that those who feel jealous or are uncharitable toward others deserve our sympathy, for they are truly unhappy. Pray for them, that their spirits will heal and that they will learn to love as Christ wants us to.

INCONVENIENCE VERSUS TRAGEDY

Men and women are sacrificed to the idols of profit and consumption: it is the "culture of waste." If a computer breaks it is a tragedy, but poverty, the needs and dramas of so many people end up being considered normal.

For today, reflect on the true tragedies of the world, and keep in proper perspective the little crises of everyday life. Consider using the money you might have spent on a new gadget or convenience to donate to a charitable organization that provides relief for the hungry and poor.

February *22*

THE LORD IS
WITH YOU

There is no cross, big or small, in our life, which the Lord does not share with us.

For today, take your worries and concerns to the Lord and ask him to guide you in finding a solution. Put it in his hands.

GOD GIVES US STRENGTH

Having faith does not mean having no difficulties, but having the strength to face them, knowing we are not alone.

For today, pray for someone who is going through a difficult time. Reach out to that person to remind him or her that God is with him or her; God will give us the strength to get through anything when we rest on his grace and help.

DIVINE LIGHT

The light of faith illumines all our relationships and helps us to live them in union with the love of Christ, to live them like Christ.

For today, try to be joyful around others, even if you don't feel like it. Let God's light shine through you and brighten the way for others.

REMAIN HOPEFUL

We ought never to lose hope. God overwhelms us with his grace, if we keep asking.

For today, ask God to help you remain hopeful in times of stress or despair. If you are struggling with something, keep asking for God's help. Remain patient, and don't lose hope.

PROTECT ALL CREATION

Let us protect Christ in our lives, so that we can protect others, so that we can protect creation!

For today, listen for God's voice, and be open to his plan for you as protector so you will be better able to make wise decisions on the behalf of your loved ones. Answer God's call to protect all his creation and the environment in which we live.

A CHRISTIAN EXAMPLE

If you happen to be with an atheist who tells you that he does not believe in God, you can read him the whole library, where it says that God exists, and where it is proven that God exists, and he will not believe. . . . If in the presence of this same atheist you witness to a consistent, Christian life, something will begin to work in his heart.

For today, don't just speak of your faith, live it. If you see someone who needs help, provide it. Open the door or carry groceries for someone who is physically challenged, generously tip a harried restaurant server, or anonymously pay the check for a young family's meal. Witness to a consistent Christian life so others may follow.

DO GOOD WORKS IN SECRET

When one performs a good work, the desire arises almost instinctively in us to be esteemed and admired for this good action, to gain satisfaction from it. Jesus calls us to perform these gestures without ostentation, and to rely solely on the reward of the Father "who sees in secret."

For today, make a donation or do an act of kindness or generosity for someone in such a way that they cannot know it came from you. Derive your happiness from the Father's reward.

MISSIONARY FAMILIES

Christian families are missionary families. . . . They are missionary also in everyday life, in their doing everyday things, as they bring to everything the salt and the leaven of faith!

For today, plan an activity with your family—or a small group of friends—to help spread God's Word and act as missionaries of the Church.

WOMEN IN THE CHURCH

I believe that we have much more to do in making explicit this role and charism of women. We can't imagine a Church without women, but women active in the Church, with the distinctive role that they play.

For today, in honor of Women's History Month, pray in thanksgiving for Bl. Mother Teresa and St. Rose Philippine Duchesne and all women throughout history who have been active in the Church and who have been living examples of God's love in the world.

CONTRIBUTIONS OF WOMEN

I encourage the contribution of so many women who work within the family, in the areas of teaching the faith, pastoral work, schooling, but also in social, cultural and economic structures.

For today, recognize the contribution of some of the women in your parish or community by sending them a congratulatory or complimentary e-mail or letter. Thank them for their service.

THE STRENGTH OF FORGIVENESS

G od's forgiveness is stronger than any sin.

For today, ask God to forgive you for past transgressions. Consider participating in the Sacrament of Penance at your church, especially if it's been a long time since your last confession.

A TROUBLED CONSCIENCE

Indifference to our neighbor and to God also represents a real temptation for us Christians. Each year during Lent we need to hear once more the voice of the prophets who cry out and trouble our conscience.

For today, resolve to allow your conscience to be troubled by prophetic wisdom during Lent and throughout the year. Put aside your indifference, and pray for those who are suffering in the world. Ask God to help you find a way to make a difference.

DON'T SHUT YOURSELF IN

We cannot keep ourselves shut up in parishes, in our communities, when so many people are waiting for the Gospel!

For today, follow the teaching of Pope Francis, and go out into the community to evangelize—by living God's love in your daily activities, discussing your faith with your children or other young people you know, supporting your neighbors, or helping someone in need.

PRIDE BREEDS LONELINESS

Take care not to place your hope in money or pride, power or vanity, because they can promise you nothing good!

For today, avoid spending too much time looking in mirrors, checking to see who has liked your Facebook posts, or thinking about your appearance. Instead, focus outwardly toward others. Ask your friends and coworkers, "How are you doing today?" and then listen.

PROCLAIM THE GOOD NEWS

Jesus sends his disciples out to all nations. To every people. . . . Jesus did not provide a short list of who is, or is not, worthy of receiving his message and his presence. Instead, he always embraced life as he saw it. In faces of pain, hunger, sickness and sin. In faces of wounds, of thirst, of weariness, doubt and pity. Far from expecting a pretty life, smartly-dressed and neatly groomed, he embraced life as he found it.

For today, as a disciple of Jesus, pray to see in people what God sees in them—their potential, their destiny in Christ, and their profound, unalterable human dignity.

WOMEN OF SERVICE

It is necessary to broaden the opportunities for a stronger presence of women in the church. . . . We have to work harder to develop a profound theology of the woman.

For today, contemplate how women have contributed to the good of the Church. Take a moment to send a note of gratitude to a woman who has given you guidance, who has served with dedication in the service of the Church, or who has been a strong model and witness to the Christian faith in your life.

MINISTERS OF MERCY

How are we treating the people of God? I dream of a church that is a mother and shepherdess. The church's ministers must be merciful, take responsibility for the people and accompany them like the good Samaritan, who washes, cleans and raises up his neighbor. This is pure Gospel. God is greater than sin.

For today, have faith in the goodness and sovereignty of God over all things, including sin. Let this sink into your heart and mind. In thanksgiving for the gift of God's goodness, choose to forgive someone today, perhaps someone who you need to forgive again. Do not keep the hurt, but give it to Jesus so that you may be released and the person who hurt or insulted you may be released.

CHANGING DIRECTION

L ent is a time to change direction, to respond to the reality of evil and poverty.

For today, ask, How would Jesus want me to respond to the evil realities in the world? What can one person do to help?

TRUE HAPPINESS

What gives us true freedom, true salvation and true happiness is the compassion, tenderness and solidarity of his love.

For today, remember that Jesus took on the burden of our sins and died for us. He comforts us and loves us as a parent loves a treasured child, enabling us to feel safe and happy. Be joyful today, confident in God's love.

FOCUS ON THE GOOD

Negativity is contagious but so is positivity; desperation is contagious but so is joy: do not follow negative people but continue to radiate light and hope around you! And know that hope doesn't disappoint, it never deludes!

For today, read or listen to the news looking for the good in people and events. Remember that journalism can be sensational when forming judgments. Search out news stories that are not on the front page—often, good news is offered but is less prominently featured.

A CONCRETE ACT

During Lent, let us find concrete ways to overcome our indifference.

For today, ask, What can I sacrifice during Lent that will enable me to help someone in need? Perhaps use the funds you save by sacrificing a special treat during Lent to donate to a food pantry.

WE NEED GOD

If we think we don't need God who reaches out to us through Christ, because we believe we can make do on our own, we are headed for a fall. God alone can truly save and free us.

For today, ask God to help you with something you've been grappling with on your own. Trust him.

TAKE A RISK

It is better to have a Church that is wounded but out in the streets than a Church that is sick because it is closed in on itself.

For today, consider participating in a new volunteer activity—something you haven't done before. Move out of your comfort zone. If you normally volunteer only in your church, look for an opportunity in the larger community.

POVERTY WITHOUT HOPE

*D*estitution is not the same as *poverty:* destitution is poverty without faith, without support, without hope.

For today, ask, Are there people in my community who are without hope? What can I do to help? In addition to donating your time or funds to the poor, consider how you can bring hope to someone in need— perhaps by simply listening or being present as a source of comfort.

BE MERCIFUL

L et us never tire, let us never tire!
He is the loving Father who always
pardons, who has that heart of mercy for
us all. And let us too learn to be merciful
to everyone.

*For today, pray for the resilience to be
merciful and kind to all—even those who
are spiteful or unpleasant. Write down the
name of one person who has hurt you in the
past, and pray for that person today.*

BE CONCERNED WITH YOUR OWN SINS

Men and women who are merciful have big, big hearts: they always excuse others and think more of their own sins. Were someone to say to them: "but do you see what so and so did?" they respond in mercy saying: "but I have enough to be concerned over with all I have done."

For today, think of a situation in which you may have hurt someone else, even if unintentionally. Consider writing or calling that person and asking forgiveness. Ask God to forgive you, too.

MODEL OF FAITH

S t. Joseph is the model . . . for all faithful, for he knew how to overcome the darkness of doubt, the experience of exile and flight from his home without ever losing his faith in God and in His Love.

For today, ask the Lord to show you how he is present and leading you forward in the midst of some difficulty you are facing. Ask Jesus for the gift of faith and confess your faith when things get difficult by saying, "Jesus, I trust in you." Resolve to keep your focus on the Lord's goodness.

HOW CAN MONEY SERVE?

M oney has to serve, not to rule!

For today, reflect on the ways you can avoid letting money rule your life, and instead use or raise money to serve others. Perhaps you can take up a collection for someone in your community who has overwhelming medical needs or collect funds for an organization that is serving victims of a natural disaster.

WOMEN WHO OPEN DOORS

Women, in the Church and on the journey of faith, had and still have today a special role in opening the doors to the Lord.

For today, endeavor to learn something new about women who have made an important and lasting contribution to the Church— perhaps Bl. Mother Teresa, Dorothy Day (social activist), or St. Katharine Drexel. If possible, share what you've learned with a daughter, granddaughter, or another young woman.

GOD IS REAL

God is a reality with a capital "R." Jesus reveals to us that this reality is a Father of infinite goodness and mercy, in relation with whom he lives.

For today, live out God's love in all you do so that you reflect the image of his goodness to others. The witness of your Christian faith—being love to others—is a great form of gratitude for the Father's own goodness to us.

DO NOT CONDEMN OTHERS

Never condemn. . . . If you want to condemn, condemn yourself. Never limp with both legs, as Elijah says, trying to take advantage of situations.

For today, ask, Am I sometimes tempted to judge others as I would not want to be judged? Consider your own transgressions rather than finding fault with other people.

POVERTY HURTS

L et us not forget that real poverty hurts: no self-denial is real without this dimension of penance. I distrust a charity that costs nothing and does not hurt.

For today, make a sacrifice that will truly inconvenience you. Perhaps abstain for a time from a food, drink, or activity you really enjoy, or consider spending your next day off from your job working in the service of others.

MAKE ROOM FOR GOD

There are no difficulties, trials, or misunderstandings to fear, provided we remain united to God as branches to the vine, provided we do not lose our friendship with him, provided we make ever more room for him in our lives.

For today, make extra room in your life for God, even if nothing is troubling you and everything is going fine. Remain in friendship with God when times are good, and he will be with you in times of trouble.

BE A SOURCE OF HOPE

A mid so much darkness, we need to see the light of hope and to be men and women who bring hope to others.

For today, write down a list of talents you possess. Then ask, How can I use one of these talents to bring hope to others? Perhaps you have a special skill that you can teach someone else. Maybe you're simply a good listener. Put your talent to work in the world and become a source of hope.

CHRISTIAN UNITY

Christian unity—we are convinced—will not be the fruit of subtle theoretical discussions. . . . When the Son of Man comes, he will find us still discussing! . . . We need to encounter one another and to challenge one another under the guidance of the Holy Spirit, who harmonizes diversities, overcomes conflicts, reconciles differences.

For today, ask the Holy Spirit to heal divisions among Christians. If you have Christian friends, family members, or colleagues, ask them sometime if they would join you in praying the Our Father when you or they are facing some difficulty or struggle.

March **28**

REFUSE TO JUDGE

Why is it so difficult to tolerate the faults of others? Have we forgotten that Jesus bore our sins?

For today, aspire to be more understanding of people in different situations than your own. Refuse to judge their hearts. Pray that all will receive the support they need and grow in God's love.

SPREAD THE WORD

How wonderful it is to proclaim to everyone the love of God which saves us and gives meaning to our lives!

For today, think about ways you can spread God's Word outside your own community. Are there global organizations to which you can contribute? If possible, consider using social media—Twitter, Facebook, or blogs— to spread your Christian joy to others around the world.

BE OPEN TO NEW IDEAS

Differences between persons and communities can sometimes prove uncomfortable, but the Holy Spirit, who is the source of that diversity, can bring forth something good from all things and turn it into an attractive means of evangelization.

For today, challenge yourself to go outside your comfort zone and learn about someone who is different from you. Ask questions and truly listen to his or her ideas. Be open to ideas you may not have considered.

GOD'S LOVE CONQUERS EVIL

J esus on the Cross feels the whole
weight of the evil, and with the force
of God's love he conquers it, he defeats it
with his resurrection.

*For today, reflect on Jesus' suffering for us.
Strive to keep the significance of Jesus' Death
and Resurrection—his victory over evil—
close to your heart.*

NEVER TIRE

Do not forget this: the Lord never tires of forgiving! It is we who tire of asking forgiveness.

For today, if you grow tired seeing yourself fall into the same sins, take courage—the Lord may allow your weakness to help you trust in his strength. He will help you. Continue to ask God for forgiveness, and trust that he is with you as you continue to seek holiness. He is proud of your efforts!

April *2*

TAKE A BREAK
FOR GOD

Sunday is the Lord's Day. Let us find time to be with him.

For today, pray for all those who must work on Sundays to provide for their families. If you too must work on Sundays, strive to take a few moments each Sunday—while eating lunch or taking a break—to spend with God.

PROTECTORS OF EARTH

It is human beings who abuse nature, constantly. We have in some sense begun to lord it over nature, sister earth, mother earth. I remember . . . what an old farmer once told me: "God always forgives, we men and women sometimes forgive, but nature never forgives." If you abuse her, she gives it back to you.

For today, thank God for those who work to save the environment, who speak about it and educate others. Read their words and learn from them what you can also do to help.

THE VOICE OF TRUTH

How many people pay dearly for their commitment to truth! Upright people who are not afraid to go against the current! How many just men prefer to go against the current, so as not to deny the voice of conscience, the voice of truth! And we, we must not be afraid!

For today, pray in thanksgiving for all who peacefully work for change and an end to injustice among peoples.

PRAY FOR THE IMPRISONED

Is there room in your heart for those who haven't fulfilled the Commandments? Who have made mistakes and are in prison? . . . If you are not in prison it is because the Lord has helped you not to fall.

For today, pray for all those who are in prison, that they may find God and have the grace to turn their lives around.

REAL POVERTY

It has been said that the only real regret lies in not being a saint; we could also say that there is only one real kind of poverty: not living as children of God and brothers and sisters of Christ.

For today, thank God for your blessings, including the gift of your faith. Count among your riches your relationship with God the Father.

UNDER THE LORD'S GAZE

How beautiful it is to stand before the Crucifix, simply to be under the Lord's gaze, so full of love.

For today, attend Mass, if possible, and spend some time before or after worship to stand before the crucifix, look up at Christ, and contemplate his love for you. If you cannot attend Mass, find some quiet time for reflection, ideally in front of a crucifix in your home.

CHRISTIANS AND POLITICS

A good Catholic meddles in politics, offering the best of himself, so that those who govern can govern. But what is the best that we can offer to those who govern? Prayer!

For today, pray for all of our elected officials, at the local, state, and federal levels, that they will be guided by Christ to make decisions based on what is fair and just for all.

TANGIBLE WITNESS

Let us all remember this: one cannot proclaim the Gospel of Jesus without the tangible witness of one's life.

For today, remember it is not enough to speak about God's Word; one must live it in his or her daily life. Strive to live God's love in everything you do today.

A PRECIOUS TREASURE

We believe in the Risen One who conquered evil and death! Let us have the courage to "come out of ourselves," to take this joy and this light to all the places of our lives! The Resurrection of Christ is our greatest certainty; he is our most precious treasure! How can we not share this treasure, this certainty, with others?

For today, endeavor to be a source of hope and light to all you encounter. Share your joy in Christ with others by lending a helping hand or by simply being available to listen.

PRAY FOR THOSE CALLED TO RELIGIOUS VOCATIONS

No vocation is born of itself or lives for itself. A vocation flows from the heart of God and blossoms in the good soil of faithful people, in the experience of fraternal love.

For today, pray for all those who are considering a religious calling, that God will guide them in making the right decision for themselves and that they will honor their calling with integrity and dignity.

NURTURE THE EARTH

The book of Genesis tells us that God created man and woman entrusting them with the task of filling the earth and subduing it, which does not mean exploiting it but nurturing and protecting it, caring for it through their work.

For today, aspire to treat our planet as our only home, God's gift of creation with which he's entrusted us. If you do not currently recycle paper and used containers, make a plan to begin doing so.

BROTHERHOOD AND SISTERHOOD

And this is true, brotherhood is beautiful! Jesus Christ also brought to its fullness this human experience of being brothers and sisters, embracing it in Trinitarian love and thereby empowering it to go well beyond the ties of kinship and enabling it to surmount every barrier of extraneousness.

For today, treat your neighbors, co-workers, and even strangers as your brothers and sisters in Christ. Treat them with the respect you would show your siblings.

REMEMBERING A SERVANT OF THE PEOPLE

The Church encourages those in power to be truly at the service of the common good of their peoples.

For today, let us remember those who have worked in the service of the common good, sometimes with great sacrifice.

PRAY FOR THE VICTIMS OF TERRORISM

To live by faith means to put our lives in the hands of God, especially in our most difficult moments.

For today, pray for victims of violence, that they are able to persevere, in spite of their injuries, and live satisfying, fulfilling lives with a strengthened faith in our Lord.

CONTEMPLATE BEAUTY

Is this the world in which we are living? Creation retains its beauty which fills us with awe and it remains a good work. But there is also "violence, division, disagreement, war." This occurs when man, the summit of creation, stops contemplating beauty and goodness, and withdraws into his own selfishness.

For today, take time to contemplate God's beauty and goodness. Go on a hike. Take a drive in a scenic area. Step outside yourself and focus on the big picture, God's creation. Be filled with awe.

GOD'S PLAN INSCRIBED IN NATURE

P lease, I would like to ask all those who have positions of responsibility in economic, political and social life, and all men and women of goodwill: let us be "protectors" of creation, protectors of God's plan inscribed in nature, protectors of one another and of the environment.

For today, pray for those who are in positions of power that enable them to make policy changes affecting the environment. Consider writing a letter to an elected official to encourage him or her to make policy decisions that protect God's creation.

INCLUDE THE EXCLUDED

M oreover, when our hearts are authentically open to universal communion, this sense of fraternity excludes nothing and no one.

For today, think of a way you might be able to include someone in an activity who might otherwise be left out. Perhaps you can provide transportation for an elderly or disabled member of your church who might otherwise not be able to attend Mass or a special function.

GIFT OF PEACE

Violence is not conquered by violence.
Lord, send us the gift of peace.

For today, pray for the survivors of violence in your community and around the world, that they are filled with peace and find a way, with God's guidance, to forgive the perpetrators of violence.

PRAY FOR AN END TO VIOLENCE

For this reason, I appeal forcefully to all those who sow violence and death by force of arms: in the person you today see simply as an enemy to be beaten, discover rather your brother or sister, and hold back your hand!

For today, pray for an end to violence in our schools and communities.

THE WORLD'S ORIGIN

The Big Bang theory, which is proposed today as the origin of the world, does not contradict the intervention of a divine creator but depends on it.

For today, aim to learn something new about science's view of the origin of the world, and consider how those ideas may reflect the Creator's plan.

April *22*

BE A GOOD STEWARD OF THE EARTH

When we speak of the "environment," what we really mean is a relationship existing between nature and the society which lives in it. Nature cannot be regarded as something separate from ourselves or as a mere setting in which we live. We are part of nature, included in it and thus in constant interaction with it.

For today, celebrate Earth Day by volunteering at a river or park cleanup event, by going out of your way to recycle paper or plastic food containers, or by attending an Earth Day celebration in your community and learning more about how you can get involved.

PITCH IN FOR ECOLOGY

Ecology is essential for the survival of mankind; it is a moral issue which affects all of us.

For today, consider additional ways you can do your part to save the environment. Perhaps you could begin carrying reusable cloth or plastic bags for your grocery purchases or install a filter on your faucet instead of buying bottled water.

CREATION IS A GIFT

Creation is not some possession that we can lord over for our own pleasure; nor, even less, is it the property of only some people, the few: creation is a gift, it is the marvelous gift that God has given us, so that we will take care of it and harness it for the benefit of all, always with great respect and gratitude.

For today, show respect for the earth by washing and reusing plastic water bottles or food containers to store items or leftover meals. Carry a reusable drink container when you are away from home instead of stopping at a store to buy soft drinks and bottled water.

GOD'S SIGNS

We are losing our attitude of wonder, of contemplation, of listening to creation. . . . Why does this happen? Why do we think and live horizontally, we have drifted away from God, we no longer read his signs.

For today, look for signs of God all around you. What does he want you to see? If possible, jot down a few words about each sign you see as you move through your day. Tonight, read your list, and ask what God's signs are telling you.

LIVING STONES

The Church is not a fabric woven of things and interests; she is the Temple of the Holy Spirit, the Temple in which God works, the Temple in which, with the gift of Baptism, each one of us is a living stone. This tells us that no one in the Church is useless. . . . No one is secondary. No one is the most important person in the Church, we are all equal in God's eyes.

For today, attend Mass, if possible, or another community function at your church. Notice the observable differences among people in the community. Consider how all of us are equal before God, in spite of our differences, and how each one of us is a living stone in the Temple of the Holy Spirit.

REACHING FULLNESS

When we read the account of Creation in Genesis we risk imagining that God was a magician, complete with an all-powerful magic wand. But that was not so. He created beings and he let them develop according to the internal laws with which He endowed each one, that they might develop, and reach their fullness.

For today, reflect on ways you have reached your potential and the ways in which you might still reach greater fullness. Consider learning something new, or revisit a talent you haven't used in a while. Take advantage of the abilities with which God has gifted you to further his Kingdom in some way.

EVOLUTION AND CREATION

Evolution in nature does not conflict with the notion of Creation, because evolution presupposes the creation of beings who evolve.

For today, give thanks for all of the world's creatures, from the smallest bacteria to the largest of animals, for God is the Creator who brought everything to life.

EASTER PRAYER

And so we ask the risen Jesus, who turns death into life, to change hatred into love, vengeance into forgiveness, war into peace.

For today, reflect on the message of Easter and our Risen Lord. Pray that those who feel hatred will experience a conversion of heart and learn to forgive. Pray for an end to all wars.

JESUS IS WITH US ALWAYS

Jesus is Lord! And he is Lord from the cross, from there he reigned. That is why . . . he can understand us: he became like us in every way. So we have a Lord who is able to weep with us, who can be at our side through life's most difficult moments.

For today, know that Jesus is with you, even when your prayers have not been answered in the way you had hoped. Instead of asking God to fix all your problems, pray for the strength to face them with Jesus.

PRAY FOR THE UNEMPLOYED

Work is part of God's loving plan, we are called to cultivate and care for all the goods of creation and in this way share in the work of creation!

For today, the feast of St. Joseph the Worker, pray for those who are unemployed or underemployed, that they may find work so they can support themselves and their families with dignity.

IN HONOR OF MOTHERS

Being a mother doesn't only mean bringing a child to the world, but it is also a life choice. What does a mother choose, what is the life choice of a mother? The life choice of a mother is the choice to give life. And this is great, this is beautiful.

For today, as Mother's Day approaches, say a prayer for the strength of mothers everywhere, for the unborn, and for your own mother and the other mothers in your life. If your mother is living, plan to do something special for her this Mother's Day.

ANTIDOTE TO INDIVIDUALISM

Mothers are the strongest antidote to the spread of self-centered individualism. "Individual" means "what cannot be divided." Mothers, instead, "divide" themselves, from the moment they bear a child to give him to the world and help him grow.

For today, give thanks for all of the good mothers who are too busy caring for their families to focus solely on themselves. Do something special and unexpected for a mother in your life today—your own or someone else's.

COMMUNICATE WITH TENDERNESS

The world of media also has to be concerned with humanity, it too is called to show tenderness. The digital world can be an environment rich in humanity; a network not of wires but of people.

For today, vow to keep the humanity in social media. Respond to others with kindness, even when doing so anonymously. If you don't use social media, discuss its proper use and etiquette with the young people in your life who do.

THE WARMTH OF HOPE

To protect creation, to protect every man and every woman, to look upon them with tenderness and love, is to open up a horizon of hope; it is to let a shaft of light break through the heavy clouds; it is to bring the warmth of hope!

For today, celebrate the warmth and promise of spring! Look upon each creature and all of your brothers and sisters as God's creations to be protected and treasured.

OUR RISEN LORD

L et the Risen Jesus enter your life,
welcome him as a friend, with trust.

For today, let the promise of Easter fill you with joy and guide you in everything you do. Take time to indulge in a friendly chat with Jesus, perhaps while outdoors or taking a walk.

THE EXAMPLE OF MOTHER CHURCH

Mother Church teaches us to give food and drink to those who are hungry and thirsty, to clothe those who are naked. And how does she do this? She does it . . . through the example of so many dads and mamas, who teach their children that what we have extra is for those who lack the basic necessities.

For today, reflect on how you can give to others to provide for their necessities. Know that, by your actions, you are teaching others what authentic love looks like.

CARE FOR THOSE WHO DEPEND ON YOU

One who does not do justice with the people who are dependent on him is not a good Christian.

For today, ask, Who depends on me? Am I doing each of them justice, or can I improve and do something better?

MAKE PEACE THROUGH DIALOGUE

It is impossible for peace to exist without dialogue. All the wars, all the strife, all the unsolved problems over which we clash are due to a lack of dialogue. When there is a problem, talk: this makes peace.

For today, resolve to talk out your problems with an estranged family member or a friend or coworker with whom you've had a disagreement. Try to find some common ground through dialogue to improve relations with that person.

BE RESPONSIBLE
FOR OTHERS

Occasionally our world forgets the special value of time spent at the bedside of the sick, since we are in such a rush; caught up as we are in a frenzy of doing, of producing, we forget about giving ourselves freely, taking care of others, being responsible for others.

For today, plan to spend some time with a friend or acquaintance who is ailing. Perhaps take him or her a special meal or another small gift. Pray for the resilience of those who are full-time caregivers for a sick child, frail spouse, or elderly parent.

A JOYFUL RELATIONSHIP

This relationship with the Lord is not intended as a duty or an imposition. It is a bond that comes from within. It is *a relationship lived with the heart*: it is our friendship with God, granted to us by Jesus, a friendship that changes our life and fills us with passion, with joy.

For today, reflect on your relationship with God: Do you sometimes regard prayer or the liturgy as a duty rather than a privileged relationship? Strive to appreciate your time in worship and prayer as an opportunity to grow in joyful friendship with the Lord.

THE ONLY GOD

Worshipping the Lord means giving Him the place that he must have; worshipping the Lord means stating, believing—not only by our words— that he alone truly guides our lives; worshipping the Lord means that we are convinced before him that he is the only God, the God of our lives, the God of our history.

For today, think of one concrete thing you can do—through action instead of words—to show that the one true God guides your life.

MAKE TIME FOR THE SICK

Charity takes time. Time to care for the sick and time to visit them. Time to be at their side.

For today, make plans to spend a day volunteering at a local health center. Call ahead to find out which volunteer activities are available. Many hospitals use volunteers to deliver and pick up food trays, help patients write e-mails or letters, or simply provide bedside visits.

RETURN TO THE LORD

Humanity is in need of justice, of peace, of love and will have it only by returning with their whole heart to God, who is the source of it all.

Today, follow the Holy Father's advice, and turn to the Lord with all your heart. To help you do that, spend ten minutes today—and every day after—reading the Gospel.

PRAY FOR THOSE WHO MAKE YOU ANGRY

A re you angry with someone? Pray for that person. That is what Christian love is.

For today, pray for someone with whom you are angry or who has angered you in the past. Ask God to help you be sincere in your prayer for that person, even if it is very difficult.

THE SEARCH FOR HAPPINESS

God has placed in the heart of every man and woman an irrepressible desire for happiness, for fulfillment.

For today, consider what makes you feel happy and fulfilled. Work toward achieving true happiness through faith in God and through trusting his plan for you.

TRANSFORMING HEARTS

The Saints were not superhuman. They were people who loved God in their hearts, and who shared this joy with others.

For today, consider the ways in which you share your Christian joy with others, and reflect on ways in which you can improve. How can these improvements help you make a difference in the world and in the hearts of others?

WISDOM OF
THE HEART

The experience of suffering can become a privileged means of transmitting grace and a source for gaining and growing in *sapientia cordis* [wisdom of the heart].

For today, reflect on a time you have suffered—perhaps from an injury, illness, or financial crisis. How did you grow in wisdom? How can you use that wisdom to help others deal with their own crises?

PROTECT THE CHILDREN

May Mary Most Holy, Mother of tenderness and mercy, help us to carry out, generously and thoroughly, our duty to humbly acknowledge and repair past injustices and to remain ever faithful in the work of protecting those closest to the heart of Jesus.

For today, consider, how can you help protect our children, those closest to the heart of Jesus. Talk with your children to ensure they know important safety advice about boundaries, trusting their instincts, and telling trusted adults about bad behavior. If you teach RCIA classes or Sunday school in your church, get training to teach children about ways to protect themselves and respond in the face of danger or indiscretion.

MOTHER MARY AND THE CHURCH

We Christians are not orphans. . . . The Church is mother. Mary is mother.

For today, pray for the Church, that she will continue to grow and that her members will continue to reach out to those in the world who need her care.

May 21

CHILDREN AND ELDERLY

Children and the elderly are the two poles of life and the most vulnerable as well, often the most forgotten.

For today, do something to support the elderly and children. Make plans to spend time by phone or in person with an older person or to help an overwhelmed mother with childcare.

GO AGAINST
THE TIDE

Go against the tide and have the daring to move precisely against the current.

For today, ask, Is there a behavior or value in today's society that Jesus would not want us to adopt? How can you counteract the popularity of that behavior for your children or grandchildren? How can you encourage them to go against the tide?

FACING CHALLENGES

We face so many challenges in life: poverty, distress, humiliation, the struggle for justice, persecutions, the difficulty of daily conversion, the effort to remain faithful to our call to holiness, and many others. But if we open the door to Jesus and allow him to be part of our lives, if we share our joys and sorrows with him, then we will experience the peace and joy that only God, who is infinite love, can give.

For today, open the door to Jesus, and invite him to help you with your problems and daily struggles. Ask for guidance in making tough decisions.

TRUE CHRISTIANS

But can't we make Christianity a little more human—they say—without the cross, without Jesus, without renunciation? In this way we would become like Christians in a pastry shop, saying: what beautiful cakes, what beautiful sweets! Truly beautiful, but not really Christians!

For today, attend Mass or spend time contemplating the Cross in front of a crucifix in your home. Take time to imagine the depth of Jesus' suffering. Do not sugarcoat it in your mind. Jesus assumed the burden of our sins and died on the Cross so that we could be saved and follow his example of love.

GOD'S MERCY IS LIMITLESS

Given the premise, and this is fundamental, that the mercy of God is limitless for those who turn to him with a sincere and contrite heart, the issue for the unbeliever lies in obeying his or her conscience. There is sin, even for those who have no faith, when conscience is not followed.

For today, recall a time when your conscience told you to do something you knew was right. Did you realize God was speaking to you through your conscience? Ask God now to forgive you for any times you did not follow your conscience and do the right thing.

RESPOND TO EVIL WITH GOOD

Sometimes it may seem as though God does not react to evil, as if he is silent. And yet, God has spoken, he has replied, and his answer is the Cross of Christ: a word that is love, mercy, forgiveness.

For today, reflect on evil in the world and how God wants us to respond to it—by taking on the cross as Jesus did. It may seem impossible in the face of evil to respond with mercy and forgiveness, but this is what God asks us to do—to fight evil with good.

SPIRITUAL THIRST

Man is like a traveler who, crossing the deserts of life, thirsts for the living water: gushing and fresh, capable of quenching his deep desire for light, love, beauty and peace. We all feel this desire! And Jesus gives us this living water: he is the Holy Spirit, who proceeds from the Father and whom Jesus pours out into our hearts.

For today, quench your spiritual thirst by opening your heart to Jesus. Pray for inner peace and for the strength to overcome obstacles on your life's journey.

BE NOT AFRAID

W e must not be afraid of being Christian and living as Christians! We must have this courage to go and proclaim the Risen Christ, for he is our peace, he made peace with his love, with his forgiveness, with his Blood and with his mercy.

For today, speak openly of your faith to whoever might be receptive—and even those who aren't. Although you may not live in an area where Christians are persecuted, it can still be difficult to speak out among others who have not accepted Christ. Summon the courage.

PEEL AWAY VANITY

Vanity is like an onion. You take it, and begin to peel it . . . and you peel away vanity today, a little bit tomorrow, and your whole life you're peeling away vanity in order to overcome it. And at the end you are pleased: I removed the vanity, I peeled the onion, but the odor remains with you on your hand.

For today, examine your conscience for signs of vanity. Have you tried to peel it away a little at a time? It can be difficult not to desire to impress others. Aspire to be less vain and more devoted to humbly following the path God has prepared for you.

SEE THE FACE OF YOUR BROTHERS AND SISTERS

You will discover that God can be "seen" also *in the face of your brothers and sisters*, especially those who are most forgotten: the poor, the hungry, those who thirst, strangers, the sick, those imprisoned (cf. Mt 25:31-46). Have you ever had this experience?

For today, remember to look for God in the face of the next homeless or needy person you encounter. If possible, help him or her by paying for a meal or groceries. Whatever you do for the poor, you are doing for Jesus!

A PURE HEART

A pure heart is necessarily one which has been stripped bare, a heart that knows how to bend down and share its life with those most in need.

For today, become poor with the poor. Share what you can with someone who has less, without condescension, in the true spirit of kindness and kinship.

BECOME HOLY

If we—all of us—accept the grace of Jesus Christ, he changes our hearts and from sinners makes us saints. To become holy, we do not need to turn our eyes away and look somewhere else, or have, as it were, the face on a holy card! No, no, that is not necessary. To become saints, only one thing is necessary: to accept the grace which the Father gives us in Jesus Christ.

For today, consider searching online for information about a saint whose life has always interested you. What do you have in common with him or her? Strive today to behave in a saintly way, opening your heart and mind to all of your brothers and sisters in Christ.

June *2*

BE AN EXAMPLE

P ay attention, my young friends: to go against the current; this is good for the heart, but we need courage to swim against the tide. . . . We Christians were not chosen by the Lord for little things; push onward toward the highest principles. Stake your lives on noble ideals, my dear young people!

For today, aim for the loftiest goals and adhere to the highest principals in your day-to-day activities. Encourage friends and family members to be brave and to go against the crowd when necessary, in order to live as Jesus wants.

BE PATIENT

We need also to be patient if we want to understand those who are different from us. People only express themselves fully when they are not merely tolerated, but know that they are truly accepted.

For today, have patience with young people or friends or family who may be struggling to live their faith. Watch out for their safety, but give them room to make their own decisions. Provide encouragement and be a good example for them through living God's love every day.

RECONCILE YOURSELF

Confessions often seem like a procedure, a formality. . . . going to confession is not like going to the dry cleaners to get a stain removed. No! It's about going to meet with our Father who pardons us, who forgives us and who rejoices.

For today, ask Jesus for forgiveness as though you were face-to-face with him. Admit to your sins and resolve to do penance. If possible, participate in the Sacrament of Penance, or consider what Jesus would ask you to do to reconcile yourself in the face of your sins.

HEAL THE WOUNDED FIRST

The thing the church needs most today is the ability to heal wounds and to warm the hearts of the faithful. . . . I see the church as a field hospital after battle. It is useless to ask a seriously injured person if he has high cholesterol and about the level of his blood sugar! You have to heal his wounds. Then we can talk about everything else.

For today, be a witness of God's mercy. Bring healing to a neighbor, a colleague, or a family member. Take a moment to support someone in need, listen attentively and without judgment to someone's struggles, offer reassurance to someone in doubt, or simply weep with those who weep.

THE RIGHT PATH

What is glorified [by the world] is success at any cost, affluence, the arrogance of power and self-affirmation at the expense of others. Jesus challenges us, young friends, to take seriously his approach to life and to decide which path is right for us and leads to true joy.

For today, consider the path you have chosen in life and the ways in which you follow in Jesus' footsteps. Have you focused more on success and earning power than on your relationship with God? If so, make plans now to rectify that.

LEAD BY EXAMPLE

We help, we lead others to Jesus with our words and our lives, with our witness. I like to recall what St. Francis of Assisi used to say to his friars: "Preach the Gospel at all times; if necessary, use words."

For today, reflect on the witness you give to others by your words and your example. Where would your witness lead others? If it would not lead to Jesus, ask the Lord for forgiveness and the strength to amend your life and be the example God wants you to be—merciful, kind, and forgiving, even to those who are not kind in return. Lead others to Jesus with your witness.

FREEDOM TO DECIDE

But what does freedom mean? It is certainly not doing whatever you want, allowing yourself to be dominated by the passions, to pass from one experience to another without discernment, to follow the fashions of the day; freedom does not mean, so to speak, throwing everything that you don't like out the window. No, that is not freedom! Freedom is given to us so that we know how to make good decisions in life! . . . This is freedom: to have the courage to make these decisions with generosity.

For today, reflect on some major decisions in your life. Did you make good decisions with generosity? Forgive yourself for past sins, ask the Lord's forgiveness, and use that knowledge to make wiser decisions in the future. Thank God for the gift of freedom, and pray for the grace to make decisions with a generous heart.

June 9

FIND A NEW WAY

In life we all make many mistakes.
Let us learn to recognize our errors
and ask forgiveness.

*For today, consider the mistakes you have
made—the things that have gone wrong
in your life. If your mistakes have hurt
someone, ask for forgiveness. How can you
use past events and the lessons learned to
create a new and better way for the future?
Pray for guidance.*

June 10

FOCUS ON GOD

Worshipping is stripping ourselves of our idols, even the most hidden ones, and choosing the Lord as the center, as the highway of our lives.

For today, vow to avoid idolizing celebrities, sports stars, and others who may have become a major focus for you. Recognize that they are God's children too, and we are all equal in his eyes. Instead, aim to make the Lord the focus of your adoration.

11

A CONSISTENT CHRISTIAN

I ask myself: Am I a Christian by fits and starts, or am I a Christian full-time? Our culture of the ephemeral, the relative, also takes its toll on the way we live our faith. God asks us to be faithful to him, daily, in our everyday life.

For today, consider aspects of your life that have been short-lived. Have you lost interest in an activity for which you once felt passion? Did your interests change? Was something else the cause? With this self-knowledge, what steps can you take to make sure you don't lose your passion for living your faith and practicing good works?

HELP FOR THE JOURNEY

This is the real journey: to walk with the Lord always, even at moments of weakness, even in our sins.

For today, recognize that your faith life is a journey and that there will be bumpy roads along the way. Trust God to help you navigate those bumps and to forgive you when you make mistakes.

A CREDIBLE WITNESS

Inconsistency on the part of pastors and the faithful between what they say and what they do, between word and manner of life, is undermining the Church's credibility.

For today, pray for the Church, that, by staying close to Jesus Christ, pastors, leaders, and the faithful live as credible witnesses to the world. Recognize that pastors and priests are wounded and imperfect, too, and that we all must strive to be more credible witnesses for the Church, to consistently speak and act as God wants us to.

PRAY FOR PEACE BETWEEN NATIONS

God's world is a world where everyone feels responsible for the other, for the good of the other. This evening, in reflection, fasting and prayer, each of us deep down should ask ourselves: Is this really the world that I desire? Is this really the world that we all carry in our hearts? Is the world that we want really a world of harmony and peace, in ourselves, in our relations with others, in families, in cities, *in* and *between* nations?

For today, reflect on the kind of world you desire. Pray for the specific forms of peace between people and between nations that your heart yearns for.

PRAY FOR FATHERS

The Church, our mother, is committed to supporting with all her strength the good and generous presence of fathers in families, for they are the irreplaceable guardians and mediators of faith in goodness, of faith in justice and in God's protection, like St. Joseph.

For today, to honor your father, say a prayer for all fathers, for your own father, and for all the fathers you know personally. If your father is living, plan to do something special for him.

June **16**

TREASURE
YOUR FAMILY

The family is the greatest treasure of any country. Let us all work to protect and strengthen this, the cornerstone of society.

For today, arrange to spend time with members of your family. If possible, plan to share a special meal or a fun and meaningful activity together.

June **17**

PRAY FOR THOSE IN POVERTY

M ay we never get used to the poverty and decay around us. A Christian must act.

For today, reflect on how those who suffer the pressures of poverty may be more tempted to despair, which may lead to incidents of violence and crime. Considers ways you can help fight poverty in the world and in your community through donations or prayer.

REDISCOVER COMMUNITY PRAYER

May each family rediscover family prayer, which helps to bring about mutual understanding and forgiveness.

For today, make a point to pray every day—in the morning, at dinner, or before bed. Consider setting aside the same time every week to pray with a friend, your family, or your community. Make it a ritual.

19

TAKE CARE OF YOUR FAMILY

Take care of your family life, giving your children and dear ones not only money, but most of all time, attention and love.

For today, think about ways you can love your family through acts and words rather than through gifts of money and material goods. If you have children, consider devoting some special time with each child, individually, every week. Ask questions, and take the time to really listen. If you have parents, siblings, or relatives around, when is the last time you spoke with them? Take the time to visit, call, or write a letter if it has been a while.

PRAY FOR REFUGEES

Our world is facing a refugee crisis . . . On this continent, too, thousands of persons are led to travel north in search of a better life for themselves and for their loved ones, in search of greater opportunities. Is this not what we want for our own children? We must . . . view them as persons, seeing their faces and listening to their stories, trying to respond as best we can to their situation.

For today, pray for those without a home and for those institutions and individuals who strive to make the world a better place for all refugees.

BEWARE OF TOO MUCH COMFORT

Beware of getting too comfortable! When we are comfortable, it's easy to forget other people.

For today, reflect on the many earthly comforts you experience each day and remember the people in the world who do not experience such benefits. Try to imagine how difficult it would be to live without a home, warm clothes, or enough food to eat. Consider skipping a meal to help you recall what it's like to feel hungry. Ask God to help you never forget those less fortunate.

June *22*

COMMUNICATE IN MANY WAYS

The desire for digital connectivity can have the effect of isolating us from our neighbors, from those closest to us. We should not overlook the fact that those who for whatever reason lack access to social media run the risk of being left behind.

For today, consider some of your friends or family members—especially older people— who may not have access to computers or social media and may be lonely. Make it a point to reach out to them in person, by letter, or by phone.

SERVING OTHERS

With us what is highest must be at the service of others. . . . And with us too, don't we have to wash each other's feet day after day? But what does this mean? That all of us must help one another.

For today, do some small act of service for another person. Don't wait until you have time to accomplish a major act of service. Little things matter—a phone call, a short visit, an e-mail or letter.

June **24**

THINK BIG!

In an age when we are constantly being enticed by vain and empty illusions of happiness, we risk settling for less and thinking small when it comes to the meaning of life. Think big instead! Open your hearts!

For today, open your heart to God's plan for you. Reflect on the talents and abilities with which you've been gifted, and consider how you can use those to brighten your world and the world around you. Think big!

DISAGREEMENT IS USEFUL

I like it when people say to me . . . "I don't see that, I disagree: that's what I think, you do as you wish." This is a real collaborator. And I have found people like this. . . . And this is good.

For today, if someone disagrees with you or offers a different opinion, stop to truly listen and consider his or her perspective. Weigh it against your own. You may still disagree, but do so more thoughtfully.

OVERCOME RESENTMENT

Prayer *unceasingly purifies the heart.* Praise and supplication to God prevents the heart from becoming hardened by resentment and selfishness.

For today, recognize that your resentment toward others is unhealthy for you. Commit yourself to forgiving someone who has hurt you or caused resentment to grow within you. Make a strong effort to overcome your resentment so you can lead a happier life.

SHORT-LIVED HAPPINESS

When we look only for success, pleasure and possessions, and we turn these into idols, we may well have moments of exhilaration, an illusory sense of satisfaction, but ultimately we become enslaved, never satisfied, always looking for more.

For today, think about what in your life will last forever. A lofty career position or material possessions—a nice home, fancy car, or expensive clothing—may give you temporary satisfaction, but they will not bring you everlasting peace and joy. Only God can do that. Ask the Holy Spirit to guide you to use material goods wisely.

CHRIST LEADS US TO GOD

Christ opened the path to us. He is like a roped guide climbing a mountain who, on reaching the summit, pulls us up to him and leads us to God.

For today, meditate on these words of Pope Francis. Envision yourself struggling up a steep mountain, sweating, working hard, as you follow the Lord. You may doubt your ability to make it—and on your own you can't—but Jesus is with you, leading you, guiding you, and protecting you at every corner and every turn. When you are weak, in times of struggle, when you have doubts, ask Jesus to lift you up.

LEARN ABOUT
STS. PETER AND PAUL

To be saints is not a privilege for the few, but a vocation for everyone.

For today, on the Solemnity of Sts. Peter and Paul, take some time to read a passage from one of St. Paul's Letters in the New Testament (to the Romans, Corinthians, Galatians, etc.), or search online for the apostles Peter and Paul, and read about their lives.

OPTIMISM VERSUS CHRISTIAN HOPE

Christian hope is not simply a desire, a wish, it is not optimism: for a Christian, hope is expectation, fervent expectation, impassioned by the ultimate and definitive fulfillment of a mystery, the mystery of God's love . . . it is the expectation of someone who is coming: it is Christ the Lord approaching ever closer to us, day by day, and who comes to bring us at last into the fullness of his communion and of his peace.

For today, decide to put all of your hope in Jesus Christ. This means trusting ultimately in him rather than in possessions, your own skill, or even your family or friends. And remember the Lord's promise, that even when you struggle, fail, or sin, all things work for the good of those who love God.

July **1**

FREEDOM OF CONSCIENCE

Jesus wants us free. And where is this freedom created? It is created in dialogue with God in the person's own conscience. . . . The conscience is the interior place for listening to the truth, to goodness, for listening to God; it is the inner place of my relationship with him, the One who speaks to my heart and helps me to discern, to understand the way I must take.

For today, be careful to respect the freedom of your friends and families to choose their beliefs and practices, even if their beliefs and practices are not Christian. Their freedom of conscience is sacred because it is there that they are called to be in dialogue with the Lord himself, who may even now be guiding them to himself.

CONFESS YOUR SINS

I am a sinner. This is the most accurate definition. It is not a figure of speech, a literary genre. I am a sinner.

For today, accept that we are all sinners in need of forgiveness. Attend your church to participate in the Sacrament of Penance, if possible, or set aside some quiet reflection time today to confess your sins and ask God for forgiveness. Consider how you might atone for your sins.

July *3*

TAKE TIME TO REST

R est opens our eyes to the larger picture and gives us renewed sensitivity to the rights of others. And so the day of rest, centered on the Eucharist, sheds it light on the whole week, and motivates us to greater concern for nature and the poor.

For today, take some time away from work, if possible, or make plans to take a day off. Don't always use your time off for personal tasks, household chores, or other fix-it projects, but rather, plan to spend that time with your family or friends, relaxing and doing something you love. Make leisure and rest a priority, especially on Sundays. Rejuvenate!

FREEDOM IN CHRIST

It will do us good to think of this . . . and to think that it is so beautiful to be children. . . . Jesus has opened the doors of his house to us, we are now at home. . . . This is the root of our courage: I am free, I am a child, the Father loves me and I love the Father.

For today, on Independence Day, as we celebrate America's political, social, and religious freedom, as a democracy, to live in pursuit of the good, remember our freedom in Christ is the source of all freedom—the freedom that comes from being children of God, free to live in righteousness, truth, and confidence.

July 5

LET CHRIST ENTER

Please, let Christ and his word enter your life; let the seed of the Word of God enter, let it blossom, and let it grow.

For today, consider some ways in which you can more fully open your daily life to the presence of Christ. Consider beginning a prayer journal. Search online for tips on making a prayer journal and getting the most out of it.

July **6**

DO NOT BE AFRAID

Do not be afraid of failure, do not be afraid of falling. In the art of walking it is not falling that matters, but not "staying fallen."

For today, think about the great dreams the Lord has given you for your life, and take a concrete leap of faith in that direction. Don't worry about failing—remember, God is for you, and he never fails. Ask God for the strength to deal with what may seem to be a failure and to get up and keep moving forward.

APPRECIATE CAREGIVERS

May we be always more grateful for the help of domestic workers and caregivers; theirs is a precious service.

For today, show gratitude for the service of caregivers, who dedicate themselves to care for the weak and weary among us. If you know someone who is a caregiver, send a note of appreciation and encouragement. If possible, offer to lend a hand or do an errand for him or her.

LIVE SIMPLY

Just as we need the courage to be happy,
we also need the courage to live simply.

*For today, ask yourself what it means to be
happy and live simply. Do you feel like you
should always be busy, rushing around and
always accomplishing a task? How can you
eliminate some of the stress in your life to
live a simpler, happier existence?*

THE VALUE OF PEOPLE

The poor are our teachers. They show us that people's value is not measured by their possessions or how much money they have in the bank.

For today, resolve to treat everyone with respect, regardless of the condition of their clothing or the size of their home. Be more aware of the potential people have to live as children of God and less observant of their spiritual, social, intellectual, or material possessions.

SINNERS IN NEED OF MERCY

We are all sinners. But God heals us with an abundance of grace, mercy and tenderness.

For today, amid faithfully striving to do good, accept that we are not perfect—we are all just sinners in need of grace. Trust in the Lord's strength when sin shows your weakness.

THE GRACE OF SALVATION

There is no sin that God cannot pardon. All we need to do is ask for forgiveness.

For today, think about what salvation means to you. Accept that we all sin and only God can save us through the forgiveness of sins.

WORLDLINESS IN THE CHURCH

God save us from a worldly Church with superficial spiritual and pastoral trappings! This stifling worldliness can only be healed by breathing in the pure air of the Holy Spirit who frees us from self-centeredness cloaked in an outward religiosity bereft of God.

For today, pray for an end to worldliness in the Church. Pray that the Holy Spirit would open the Church to pastoral concern for the needy and free it from any superficial focus on appearances.

SOURCE OF JOY

The Bible, [you are] not to place it on a shelf, but to keep it at hand, to read it often, every day, both individually and together, husband and wife, parents and children, maybe in the evening, especially on Sundays. This way the family grows, walks, with the light and power of the Word of God!

For today, think about setting aside time each evening, if possible, or once or twice a week to read the Bible. If you are a parent with children at home, search in advance for a parable or some passages you want to share with your children, read the passage together, and construct a simplified explanation or be prepared to answer questions about the Scripture.

LIFE'S BURDENS

L ife is often wearisome, and many times tragically so. We have heard this recently. . . . Work is tiring; looking for work is exhausting. And finding work today requires much effort. But what is most burdensome in life is not this: what weighs more than all of these things is a lack of love.

For today, if you know someone who is unemployed or unhappy in his or her work, lend a sympathetic ear to listen to his or her struggles. Pray that he or she find appropriate work soon. If possible, offer to help in some small way, such as with resume assistance or the job search.

PRAY FOR FAMILIES

Come to me, families from around the world—Jesus says—and I will give you rest, so that your joy may be complete. Take home this Word of Jesus, carry it in your hearts, share it with the family.

For today, pray for your family and families around the world who carry heavy burdens. Bring the cares of your own family to the Lord and lean on him. If you have children, teach them how to bring their worries to the Lord in prayer.

PRAY FOR NEWLY MARRIED COUPLES

And that is what marriage is! Setting out and walking together, hand in hand, putting yourselves in the Lord's powerful hands. Hand in hand, always and for the rest of your lives.

For today, pray for all married couples and anyone you know personally who is newly married or contemplating marriage, that Christ will be a source of strength and joy throughout their marriage.

FIGHT THE DEVIL

In this generation, like so many others, people have been led to believe that the devil is a myth, a figure, an idea, the idea of evil. But the devil exists and we must fight against him.

For today, recognize the fingerprints of the Devil when you are tempted to sin. Aspire to fight against him by opening your heart to Jesus and choosing good over evil every time, even in challenging situations.

FORGIVENESS IN THE FAMILY

This is important! To know how to forgive one another in families because we all make mistakes, all of us! Sometimes we do things which are not good and which harm others. It is important to have the courage to ask for forgiveness when we are at fault in the family.

For today, consider a recent situation in which you may have spoken to a family member in anger or done something hurtful. If you did not apologize at the time, do so now and ask for forgiveness. Resolve to never say goodbye or good night in anger.

SHOW MERCY

A little mercy makes the world less cold and more just.

For today, show mercy to those who have hurt or angered you or toward whom you harbor resentment. Show through your actions that you do not carry a grudge. Aim to forgive them from your heart, even if they do not apologize for their actions.

July *20*

TRANSFORM
YOUR FAITH

Take care of your relationships with others, transforming faith into life and words into good works, especially for the most needy.

For today, endeavor to be a Christian of action, not just words. Contemplate some ways you can volunteer or be of service to the needy within your community in the coming weeks.

A PLACE FOR MOTIVATION

The confessional is not a torture chamber, but the place in which the Lord's mercy motivates us to do better.

For today, consider participating in the Sacrament of Penance this week if you haven't confessed for some time. If you are uncomfortable with it, focus on ways in which you can receive God's grace through the sacrament. Encourage friends or family members to accompany you and participate as well.

ADVICE FOR THE YOUNG

You young people are brave adventurers! If you allow yourselves to discover the rich teachings of the Church on love, you will discover that Christianity does not consist of a series of prohibitions which stifle our desire for happiness, but rather a project for life capable of captivating our hearts.

For today, pray for all of the young people, that they will find in Christianity a path of love that burns in their hearts.

YOUNG PEOPLE IN THE CHURCH

L et us encourage the generosity which is typical of the young and help them to work actively in building a better world. Young people are a powerful engine for the Church and for society.

For today, peruse your parish bulletin for activities that might appeal to young people in your life. Encourage them to become involved in the Church and to put their youthful energy and creative ideas to work! Show your support and gratitude for their contribution.

THE SPIRITUAL LIFE OF OTHERS

Religion has the right to express its opinion in the service of the people, but God in creation has set us free: it is not possible to interfere spiritually in the life of a person.

For today, refrain from judging others who are searching for God, even if they hold different beliefs from yours or behave in ways with which you do not agree. Concern yourself instead with strengthening your own relationship with God.

GOD'S BEAUTY

Mankind thinks, feels, makes, but is in such need today of beauty.

For today, take time to enjoy the natural world. Look for God's beauty everywhere—in a morning sunrise, in a summer rain shower, in the colors of a wildflower.

VALUE THE GRANDPARENTS' ROLE IN A FAMILY

The great human family is like a forest, where sound trees bear solidarity, communion, trust, support, security, happy sobriety, friendship. . . . And this is why the presence of grandparents is very important: a precious presence both for practical help, and above all for their educational contribution. Grandparents preserve in themselves the values of a people, of a family, and they help parents pass them on to the children.

For today, invite your children or other young people you know to communicate with their grandparents in person or by e-mail or phone. If you are a grandparent, reach out to each of your grandchildren and express your confidence in their future.

CHRIST'S INFINITE RESERVE

What comes to mind is the miracle of the multiplication of the loaves: for you too, the Lord can multiply your love and give it to you fresh and good each day. He has an infinite reserve!

For today, ask the Lord to multiply your love—for your spouse and children, if you're married, or for friends or family members— and to help you find ways to keep it fresh, never growing stale or old.

NOURISHMENT FOR THE WEAK

The Eucharist, although it is the fullness of sacramental life, is not a prize for the perfect but a powerful medicine and nourishment for the weak.

For today, attend Mass and accept the Body and Blood of Jesus, if you are able. Surrender your heart to him, and know you are welcome at his table because of your weakness, not in spite of it.

BE CAREFUL
HOW YOU SPEAK

Take care of your speech, purifying your language of offensive words, of vulgarity and of decadent worldly expressions.

For today, resolve to avoid the use of curse words or other offensive language, even in stressful situations. Encourage your family members and friends to do the same. Be a shining example of Christ's light in the world through your words.

ALL ARE EQUAL BEFORE GOD

We continue to tolerate some considering themselves more worthy than others.

For today, pray for those who hold themselves above others, that they may realize we are all God's children and equal in his eyes.

LET EVERY VOICE BE HEARD

How important it is that the voice of every member of society be heard, and that a spirit of open communication, dialogue and cooperation be fostered.

For today, pray for dialogue between people of different races and cultures throughout the world and in your community. Look for ways you can speak and act on behalf of those whose voices are unheard, dismissed, or trivialized—even if it just means challenging one-sided views around you.

JOURNEY WITH THE CROSS

When we journey without the Cross, when we build without the Cross, when we profess Christ without the Cross, we are not disciples of the Lord, we are worldly: we may be bishops, priests, cardinals, popes, but not disciples of the Lord.

For today, pray for the courage to walk in the presence of the Lord, with the cross, to profess the crucified Christ.

PRAY FOR PRIESTS

B e close to your priests with affection and with your prayers, that they may always be shepherds according to God's heart.

For today, pray for your parish priest and for all leaders of church ministries, that they will serve God with integrity. Consider getting to know your priest or pastor on a personal level by inviting him to dinner with your family or friends.

CARE FOR THOSE WHO SUFFER

Like the Good Samaritan, may we not be ashamed of touching the wounds of those who suffer, but try to heal them with concrete acts of love.

For today, reflect on the suffering of someone you know or have heard about who is dealing with a difficult situation. If possible, do something special and unexpected for that person.

GOD HAS PATIENCE

God always has patience, patience with us, he understands us, he waits for us, he does not tire of forgiving us if we are able to return to him with a contrite heart.

For today, reflect on something you did a long time ago—perhaps years ago—that you're sorry for. Did you ever confess your sin and ask God's forgiveness? He is waiting for you to do that now, so he can pour out his mercy on you.

BE HUMBLE IN YOUR SEARCH FOR GOD

If one has the answers to all the questions—that is the proof that God is not with him. It means that he is a false prophet using religion for himself. The great leaders of the people of God, like Moses, have always left room for doubt. You must leave room for the Lord, not for our certainties; we must be humble.

For today, faithfully continue to seek God's face—never assume the quest is over and that you have all the answers. Accept the challenge to keep seeking him every day of your life.

LET PEACE BEGIN WITH ME

What a beautiful day it shall be, when weapons are dismantled in order to be transformed into tools for work! What a beautiful day that shall be! And this is possible! Let us bet on hope, on the hope for peace, and it will be possible!

For today, let the peace that the world needs begin within your own heart. Know that your efforts do matter and can have impact beyond what you may know.

A MEASURE OF UNCERTAINTY

The risk in seeking and finding God in all things, then, is the willingness to explain too much, to say with human certainty and arrogance: "God is here." We will find only a god that fits our measure.

For today, recognize that God continually surprises us and that attempting to describe God in specific words to fit our perception of him is limited. Seek to know God with a contemplative attitude of wonder.

SEARCH FOR LOST SHEEP

We should not simply remain in our own secure world, that of the ninety-nine sheep who never strayed from the fold, but we should go out, with Christ, in search of the one lost sheep, however far it may have wandered.

For today, reach out to a friend or acquaintance who has left the Church or who has perhaps lost faith. Offer to talk about his or her spiritual struggles, but don't push. Be an example of Christian patience and understanding.

WHAT CAN YOU DO TO FIGHT INJUSTICE?

We must not believe the Evil One when he tells us that there is nothing we can do in the face of violence, injustice and sin.

For today, close your ears to the Devil, who wants you to passively accept the evil in the world and do nothing in response. Rather, look for ways you can act as peacemaker in your community or in the world to fight injustice, oppression, and violence.

GOD'S GRACE

Mary, give us the grace of being joyful as we walk in the freedom of the children of God.

For today, think about someone you know who seems to be filled with grace. What about them gives you that impression? Pray today for Mary's intervention to obtain for you the grace you need.

JOY OF THE ENCOUNTER

Ours is not a joy born of having many possessions, but from having encountered a Person, Jesus, in our midst.

For today, find joy in Jesus' presence as he accompanies you throughout the day. Revel in his friendship.

August **12**

SMALL GESTURES
OF PEACE

It isn't necessary to call the United Nations to come to the house and make peace. A little gesture is sufficient. . . . And tomorrow, begin again.

For today, strive to treat each member of your family with kindness, even when angry. At the end of the day, if there has been resentment, surrender your hurts to the Lord, and surrender your relationships to him. Ask for forgiveness for your offenses, and forgive others for theirs.

THE MEASURE OF FAITH

Remember this: love is the measure of faith. How much do you love?

For today, meditate on the meaning of the Holy Father's words. How well do you love God—and how well do you love your neighbor? That is the measure of your faith.

A CHALLENGING JOURNEY

Never give way to discouragement! Ours is not a joy born of having many possessions, but from having encountered a Person: Jesus, in our midst; it is born from knowing that with him we are never alone, even at difficult moments, even when our life's journey comes up against problems and obstacles that seem insurmountable, and there are so many of them!

For today, reflect on the difficult times in your life, the many obstacles and challenges you have overcome. How did God make his presence known to you at those times? How did you grow through those challenges? Thank the Lord for his grace to overcome.

THE ASSUMPTION OF MARY

M ary's journey to heaven began with the "yes" spoken in Nazareth in response to the Heavenly Messenger's announcement of God's will to her. And in reality it is just like this: every "yes" to God is a step toward Heaven, toward eternal life. Because this is what the Lord wants: that all his children may have life in abundance! God wants us all with him, in his house!

For today, pay close attention to what the Lord is saying to you in your heart, and live out your "yes" to him! Take joy in knowing that as you let Jesus work through you and for you, you grow closer to Heaven and bring Heaven down to earth.

TIME-WASTING ACTIVITIES

Perhaps many teenagers and young people waste too much time in futile activities: chatting on the Internet or on mobile phones, watching soap operas on TV, technological progress that should simplify and improve the quality of life, but sometimes distracts you from what is really important.

For today, reevaluate how you spend your leisure. Do you use your phone or social media so much that you don't have time for personal contact? Do you watch so much TV that you don't have time to read a good book? Make it a point to carefully guard your time from being distracted by excessive entertainment consumption.

TRY NEW THINGS

God is not afraid of new things.

For today, try something new! God wants you to use your talents and abilities well. What have you always wanted to learn to do? God is not afraid to try new things, and neither should you be. Ask the Holy Spirit to guide you if there is some new way the Lord wants you to use your talents.

BRING HOPE

Today too, amid so much darkness, we need to see the light of hope and to be men and women who bring hope to others.

For today, in light of so much tragedy and evil in the world, aim to be a light of hope. If you use social media, use it to send out messages of peace and good will. Respond to others online and in person with kindness.

THE CARESS OF A GRANDPARENT

One of the most beautiful aspects of family life, of our human life as a family, is caressing a baby and being caressed by a grandfather and a grandmother.

For today, if you have grandchildren, plan to spend time with them soon. Call them often. Be a good listener. Pass out lots of hugs. Make time for your parents and grandparents if they are living. Don't let them be an afterthought in your life or in the lives of your children.

EMBRACE CHANGE

I f the Christian is a restorationist, a legalist, if he wants everything clear and safe, then he will find nothing. Tradition and memory of the past must help us to have the courage to open up new areas to God.

For today, realize the Church has undergone changes and will continue to grow. Be open to new ways of doing things as they come about, and ask how you can help make the transition easier for others.

LET GOD'S MERCY TRANSFORM YOU

Let us be renewed by God's mercy, let us be loved by Jesus, let us enable the power of his love to transform our lives too; and let us become agents of this mercy, channels through which God can water the earth, protect all creation and make justice and peace flourish.

For today, aspire to be a channel through which God's love flows. Ask God to work through you and let his mercy transform your life and increase your faith.

BE A LIGHT IN
THE WORLD

To change the world we must be good to those who cannot repay us.

For today, perform a good work for which you will receive no payment. Perhaps a young student needs help with homework or an elderly neighbor needs assistance with yard work. Be a light in the world that can help bring about change.

SEEK OUT THOSE WHO NEED HELP

We cannot become starched Christians, those over-educated Christians who speak of theological matters as they calmly sip their tea. No! We must become courageous Christians and go in search of the people who are the very flesh of Christ.

For today, consider ways you can step out of your comfort zone and seek those who need help. If possible, consider joining a mission trip with members of your parish. Or look for other outreach opportunities within your parish or community.

August **24**

TRUST THE LORD

I t is important to have friends we can trust. But it is essential to trust the Lord, who never lets us down.

For today, give thanks for your trustworthy friends, and try to be a trustworthy friend to others. But, more importantly, give thanks to the Lord for his faithful love.

August *25*

A CHURCH FOR
THE POOR

Ｈow I would like a Church which is poor and for the poor!

For today, pray for the Church, that it would be poor in spirit and never lose sight of its mission to help the poor. Pray for our world, which places more emphasis on failing banks or the latest celebrity debacle than on the tragedy of physical and moral hunger.

JOYFUL CHRISTIANS

I cannot imagine a Christian who does not know how to smile. May we joyfully witness to our faith.

For today, smile and be a joyful Christian—knowing the hope that lies before you in Jesus Christ. Live out God's love, and aim to spread that joy and happiness to everyone you meet.

A BEAUTIFUL LIFE

Let us not be satisfied with a mediocre life. Be amazed by what is true and beautiful, what is of God!

For today, reflect on the amazing and beautiful things God has done in your life, and write some of them down. The next time you are having a bad day or experiencing doubts, pull out your list and reread it.

RESPECT GOD'S WORK

A Christian who doesn't safeguard creation, who doesn't make it flourish, is a Christian who isn't concerned with God's work, that work born of God's love for us.

For today, consider ways you can show your appreciation for God's work by helping to safeguard our environment. Consider how you can be a good steward of goods and resources and what you can do to protect God's creation your daily life.

BUILDING PEACE

B uilding peace is difficult, but living without peace is a constant torment.

For today, pray for peace and justice among people throughout the world. Pray for an end to terrorism and war, and pray for forgiveness and reconciliation between nations.

WOMEN AND FAITH

Remember where your faith comes from, who gave it to you, the Holy Spirit, through your mother and grandmother . . . the beautiful work of mothers and grandmothers, the beautiful service of those women who act as mothers and the women in the family—she might even be a housekeeper, maybe an aunt—in passing on the faith.

For today, recall how your own mother or grandmother may have passed on the gift of faith. As a Christian model, how are you passing on the faith to your own children or to others? If you have children yourself, think of some concrete actions you (and your spouse) can take to raise your family in a faith-filled home.

August **31**

GIVE THANKS
FOR TEACHERS

Thank you to all teachers: educating is an important mission, which draws young people to what is good, beautiful and true.

For today, as the school year begins, pray for teachers, that they will serve with compassion, patience, and integrity. Give thanks to God for their devotion.

THE PROMISE OF YOUTH

Our generation will show that it can rise to the promise found in each young person when we know how to give them space. This means that we have to create the material and spiritual conditions for their full development; to give them a solid basis on which to build their lives; to guarantee their safety and their education to be everything they can be.

For today, reflect on how to be supportive and understanding of youth. Model for them the correct path by living a life of service, support, and understanding. If possible, volunteer at a local church youth group or community youth association.

September *2*

DO YOUR BEST WORK

Take care of your work, performing it with enthusiasm, with humility, with skill, with passion, with a mind that knows how to thank the Lord.

For today, in honor of Labor Day this month, do your work to the best of your abilities and pray for the unemployed. Thank God for the gift of employment, or if you are out of work, ask for his guidance in finding a job.

September *3*

LOOK OUT
FOR OTHERS

At times we can be self-absorbed. Lord, help us to open our hearts to others and to serve those who are most vulnerable.

For today, try to put everyone else you meet before yourself. Small things matter. Hold open the door for the person behind you, help someone get an item off the upper shelf at the grocery store, buy lunch for the homeless person on the sidewalk. Find small ways to put others' needs ahead of your own.

September 4

THE VALUE OF WORK

I t is a form of suffering, the shortage of
work—that leads you—excuse me if I
am coming [off] a little strong but I am
telling the truth—to feel that you are
deprived of dignity!

*For today, choose one aspect of your work,
and strive to improve your skill in that
area. Remember that even God worked
masterfully for six long days when he made
all of creation. Pray for those who are
looking for work, that they may find the
strength to maintain their sense of dignity
and confidence throughout the process.*

PUT FAITH INTO ACTION

One might say "I'm a serious Catholic, Father, it's really gratifying. . . . I always go to Mass, every Sunday, I take Communion." . . . "Okay. But how is your relationship with your employees? Do you pay them under the table? Do you pay them a fair wage? Do you make contributions for their pension? For their health and social security?"

For today, ask, Do I live my faith in my daily life? Does my faith show in how I treat my co-workers, my employees, or my subordinates?

LEARN FROM PERSONS WITH DISABILITIES

A motor, sensory or mental limitation can be a reason for closing in on ourselves, but it can also become, thanks to the love of parents, siblings, and friends, an *incentive to openness, sharing and ready communication with all.*

For today, learn more about the experience of someone with a disability. If you know someone with a disability, whether a child or an adult, step outside your comfort zone and ask them about the struggle— and go beyond that—amid the struggle, what are his or her other hopes, struggles, frustrations, and dreams?

LOOK FOR GOD

God is always a surprise, so you never know where and how you will find him. You are not setting the time and place of the encounter with him. You must, therefore, discern the encounter. Discernment is essential.

For today, try to be open to encounters with God in unexpected places and ways. Look for him in everyday interactions—with the grocery store clerk, the gas station attendant, a bus driver, neighbor, or in a smile or nod from a passing stranger. Appreciate his bounty in the rain, his glory in the sun, and his rest in the night.

ASK MARY TO GUIDE YOU

Victory is for those who continually arise without being discouraged. If we imitate Mary, we cannot keep our arms folded, only complaining, or perhaps dodging the hard work that others do and which is our responsibility.

For today, on the Nativity of the Blessed Virgin Mary, ask her for guidance in completing difficult tasks throughout the day. Do not be afraid to humbly put in the hard work necessary to solve important problems at work, in the community, and in the world—remember, with God, all things are possible.

ASK FOR GRACE

Let us ask the Lord for the grace to have sincere faith, a faith which is not negotiated according to the opportunities that are presented.

For today, ask the Lord to strengthen your faith in him. When life gets hectic and your days are overflowing with activity, keep your spiritual eyes fixed on Jesus, and your faith in him will keep you grounded and at peace.

September **10**

AVOID CYNICISM; TAKE ACTION

Let us not fall into humiliating indifference or a monotonous routine that prevents us from discovering what is new! Let us ward off destructive cynicism! Let us open our eyes and see the misery of the world, the wounds of our brothers and sisters who are denied their dignity, and let us recognize that we are compelled to heed their cry for help!

For today, take a break from your work or chores to notice what is happening in the world. Read the news with an open mind and an open heart; consider one way in which you might help a brother or sister in need through a donation, action, or prayer.

PRAY FOR THOSE WHO LOST THEIR LIVES ON 9/11

Let us implore from on high the gift of commitment to the cause of peace. Peace in our homes, our families, our schools and our communities. Peace in all those places where war never seems to end. Peace for those faces which have known nothing but pain. Peace throughout this world which God has given us as the home of all and a home for all. Simply PEACE.

For today, pray for the conversion of hearts, that all people may use peaceful means to attain their legitimate interests. Remember those who have lost their lives to terrorism and violence, and pray for the families and communities that have suffered from this devastation.

GOD IS LOVE

Saying that one can kill in the name of God is blasphemy.

For today, pray for the conversion of those who kill in God's name—and remember that Jesus gave his life for sinners. Pray that the Prince of Peace would come to reign in their hearts. Try also to keep your own anger in check so that peace would reign in your own heart more deeply.

HATRED OFFENDS GOD

All this gravely offends God and humanity. Hatred is not to be carried in the name of God. War is not to be waged in the name of God.

For today, pray for all people and governments to realize how greatly violence offends God, and to wage peace and love, not war.

THE IMPORTANCE OF HUMAN DIGNITY

As religious leaders, we are obliged to denounce all violations against human dignity and human rights. . . . As such, any violence which seeks religious justification warrants the strongest condemnation because the Omnipotent is the God of life and peace.

For today, have courage to condemn violations against human rights and human dignity that may be in your community or city. You need not be a religious leader to assume the duty to speak out against hatred.

September **15**

GIVE OF YOURSELF

L ord, teach us to step outside ourselves.
Teach us to go out into the streets and
manifest your love.

*For today, aim to move out of your
comfort zone and focus more on others
than on yourself. How can you make a
positive impact?*

16

CELEBRATE THE YOUNG AND THE OLD

Caring for our little ones and for our elders is a choice for civilization. And also for the future, because the little ones, the children, the young people will carry society forward by their strength, their youth, and the elderly people will carry it forward by their wisdom, their memory, which they must give to us all.

For today, consider your attitude toward the elderly. Do you sometimes not notice the elderly? Take care to give special respect to the elderly persons you meet in your day to day life, and take the time to reach out to elderly family members—listen to them, learn from them, and honor them.

TREASURE THE ELDERLY

Sometimes we cast the elderly aside, but they are a precious treasure: to cast them aside is an injustice and an irreparable loss.

For today, resolve to set aside a block of time on the same day each week to visit an elderly relative. Mark it on your calendar, and plan to keep the appointment. Or, if you have no elderly relatives nearby, look for ways to reach out to older persons in your church or local community.

WISDOM OF THE AGED

But let me ask you: Do you listen to your grandparents? Do you open your hearts to the memories that your grandparents pass on? Grandparents are like the wisdom of the family, they are the wisdom of a people.

For today, ask older family members to tell you about their lives and the lessons they've learned. Listening is the foundation of communication. Older persons have acquired much wisdom that we can receive from them.

RECEIVE PEACE

Peace is a gift of God which today too must find hearts willing to receive it and to toil to be builders of reconciliation and peace.

For today, open your heart to God's gift of peace. Pray for others to receive the same gift.

FAIRNESS AND GENEROSITY

M en and women have faith, but split the Tablets of the Law: "Yes, I do this."—"But do you give alms?"—"Yes, I always send a check to the Church."— "Okay. But at your Church, at your home, with those who depend on you, whether they are your children, your grandparents, your employees, are your generous, are you fair? . . . [You cannot] make offerings to the Church on the shoulders of injustice."

For today, reflect on how you treat those who depend on you. Do you always try to be fair, generous, and evenhanded? If not, what steps can you take to correct this?

THE ROOT OF PEACE

P rayer is at the root of peace.

*For today, pray for peace in your country,
throughout the world, and in your heart.
Trust in the power of prayer to achieve
great things.*

September *22*

LET GO OF NEGATIVITY

L et us ask the Lord for the grace not to
speak badly of others, not to criticize,
not to gossip, but rather to love everyone.

*For today, pause before you speak—avoid
the temptation to cut down someone else.
Let go of negative thoughts for greater health
and happiness.*

WATCH OUT FOR GOSSIP

The disease of gossiping, grumbling and back-biting. . . . It is the disease of cowardly persons who lack the courage to speak out directly, but instead speak behind other people's backs. . . . Brothers, let us be on our guard against the terrorism of gossip!

For today, aspire to not indulge in—or even listen to—gossip. Encourage others to avoid gossip by refusing to participate. If you need to confront a problem or a situation, take courage and do so directly—the Lord is with you always.

TAKE CARE OF STRANGERS

Take care of weakest brothers and sisters . . . Namely, take care of the elderly, the sick, the hungry, the homeless and foreigners because we will be judged on this.

For today, aim to help at least one stranger, not because of how it makes you feel, but because it is the right thing to do. Even the smallest actions can help make the world a better place.

THE POWER OF APOLOGY

Peace is made each day in the family: "Please forgive me," and then you start over. Please, thank you, sorry! . . . Let us say these words in our families! To forgive one another each day!

For today, take care to admit when you have made an error. Ask forgiveness from those you love, even if pride makes you want to stay silent.

FAMILY COURTESY

How many times do you say thank you to your wife, . . . to your husband? How many days go by without uttering this word, thanks! And the last word: sorry. We all make mistakes and on occasion someone gets offended in the marriage, in the family, and sometimes—I say—plates are smashed, harsh words are spoken but please listen to my advice: don't ever let the sun set without reconciling.

For today, remember that sometimes it takes real courage to say thank you or I'm sorry, even within our own families. We are all imperfect, but we are all worthy of forgiveness, and forgiving others shows our great dignity as children of the merciful Father.

CELEBRATE FAMILY

The life of a family is filled with beautiful moments: rest, meals together, walks in the park or the countryside, visits to grandparents. . . . But if love is missing, joy is missing, nothing is fun. Jesus always gives us that love: he is its endless source.

For today, organize a fun outing with your family sometime soon. Plan to begin your outing with a family prayer of thanksgiving to Jesus for being a loving presence in your daily lives.

THE PERFECT FAMILY

The perfect family does not exist, nor a perfect husband or wife . . . We sinners exist. Jesus, who knows us well, teaches us a secret: don't let a day end without asking forgiveness, without peace returning to our home, to our family.

For today, if you find yourself in conflict with a loved one, don't say good night or goodbye without first making peace, even if it means asking forgiveness.

THE GIFT OF COMMUNICATION

The great challenge facing us today is to *learn once again how to talk to one another*, not simply how to generate and consume information.

For today, be truly present to those you talk to—discern their needs in that moment. Do they need you to support them, to stand against negative thoughts, or simply to give them space and not add to their burdens? Be thoughtful of their needs.

PRAYER KEEPS A FAMILY STRONG

The husband for his wife, the wife for her husband, both together for their children, the children for their grandparents . . . praying for each other. This is what it means to pray in the family and it is what makes the family strong: prayer.

For today, pray for your family, and pray as a family. Set aside the same block of time each day to do this, so that you will not let the opportunity slide by.

RESPECT LIFE

Every child who, rather than being born, is condemned unjustly to being aborted, bears the face of Jesus Christ, bears the face of the Lord.

For today, as we begin Respect Life Month, pray for all unborn children, that their parents will have the courage to choose life.

THE FACE OF CHRIST

A nd every elderly person, even if he is ill or at the end of his days, bears the face of Christ. They cannot be discarded.

For today, remember that respect for life involves more than caring for the unborn; it means respect for all life, including the elderly and infirm. Pray for the elderly who are ill or lonely, that they may find peace and companionship through their relationship with God and others.

RESPECT THE VULNERABLE

Even the weakest and most vulnerable, the sick, the old, the unborn and the poor, are masterpieces of God's creation, made in his own image, destined to live forever, and deserving of the utmost reverence and respect.

For today, consider how you show respect for the vulnerable among us. If possible, plan an outing to a retirement center, a soup kitchen, or a food pantry, and let your behavior toward others be an example.

ST. FRANCIS OF ASSISI, MAN OF PEACE

That is how the name came into my heart: Francis of Assisi. For me, he is the man of poverty, the man of peace, the man who loves and protects creation; these days we do not have a very good relationship with creation, do we? He is the man who gives us this spirit of peace, the poor man.

For today, on the feast day of St. Francis of Assisi, spend some time in the outdoors, if possible, in praise of God's creation. If you have pets, thank God for their loving devotion.

October *5*

SPEAK UP FOR
THE EARTH

All peoples of the earth, all men and women of good will—all of us must raise our voices in defense of these two precious gifts: peace and nature or Sister Mother Earth as St. Francis of Assisi called her.

For today, speak out in some small way in defense of nature. Research policies regarding recycling or cleanup sites in your community and write a letter to your elected official in support of good environmental programs.

SEEK GOD IN EVERY LIFE

You can, you must try to seek God in every human life. Although the life of a person is a land full of thorns and weeds, there is always a space in which the good seed can grow. You have to trust God.

For today, strive to find the good in every person you encounter. Look for the face of God in their faces. Refrain from judging, and trust God to find a way into each person's heart.

CHERISH THE CHILDREN

In the Gospel, Jesus welcomes children, he embraces them and blesses them. . . . We need to see each child as a gift to be welcomed, cherished and protected.

For today, pray for single mothers and for any woman who is pregnant and scared, and for children and young adults who live in difficult home situations. Consider one way you can help—through Big Brothers Big Sisters of America, Birthright, or Catholic Charities centers for pregnant women.

FEED THE HUNGRY

I n a world where there is such great wealth, so many resources for giving food to everyone, it is impossible to understand how there could be so many hungry children.

For today, collect canned goods and extra food from your pantry, and deliver them to a food pantry. If your parish or local food pantry sponsors an Adopt-a-Family program for the upcoming holidays, sign up and begin to gather your donations.

October **9**

GOD IS IN EVERYONE'S LIFE

I have a dogmatic certainty: God is in every person's life. God is in everyone's life. Even if the life of a person has been a disaster, even if it is destroyed by vices, drugs or anything else—God is in this person's life.

For today, if you know someone who is struggling with drugs, alcohol, or other addictions, pray to see how God's grace is working in his or her life. Be supportive, and encourage him or her in efforts to overcome the addiction.

EVALUATE YOUR MOTIVES

A t times it seems that we are repeating today what happened at Babel: division, the incapacity to understand one another, rivalry, envy, egoism. What do I do with my life? Do I create unity around me? Or do I cause division, by gossip, criticism, or envy? What do I do? Let us think about this.

For today, follow the advice of our Holy Father, and ask these tough questions of yourself. Do you promote unity among friends or in the workplace, or have you caused rifts? How can you aim to be a better Christian in the future?

THE TREASURE OF LOVE

In each one of you there is a chest, a box, and inside there's a treasure. Your job is to open the chest and pull out the treasure, make it grow, give it to others, and receive the treasure of others.

For today, consider how you can grow the treasure of your love—through prayer, service, and opening yourself to God. Don't wait for it to keep growing before you give it to others; the sooner you give love, the sooner you will receive it.

12

A VOICE FOR PEACE

Peace is a gift of God, but requires our efforts. Let us be people of peace in prayer and deed.

For today, ask, How can I be a voice for peace, and how can I make myself heard?

CHOOSE LIFE

Too often, as we know from experience, people do not choose life, they do not accept the "Gospel of Life" but let themselves be led by ideologies and ways of thinking that block life, that do not respect life, because they are dictated by selfishness, self-interest, profit, power and pleasure, and not by love, by concern for the good of others.

For today, let your heart be life-giving to others in the world. Look for simple ways to help a life-giving or life-saving cause or to help someone who is struggling under life's burdens.

DON'T WASTE FOOD

Let us remember well, however, that whenever food is thrown out it is as if it were stolen from the table of the poor, from the hungry! I ask everyone to reflect on the problem of the loss and waste of food.

For today, recycle food at home by finding creative ways to use your leftovers in your next meal. If you dine out, don't leave food on your plate—ask for a takeout container. If your organization, church, or place of work has an event with food, donate any leftovers to a food bank or to an organization that feeds the hungry. Teach your children not to waste food.

AN INTERIOR PILGRIMAGE

I invite you to immerse yourself in the joy of the Gospel and nurture a love that can light up your vocation and your mission. I urge each of you to recall, as if you were making an interior pilgrimage, that first love with which the Lord Jesus Christ warmed your heart, not for the sake of nostalgia but in order to persevere in joy.

For today, reflect on your life and growth as a Christian. Think about when you first began to know Jesus and how it changed your life and helped you grow in grace and love.

SHARE YOUR ABUNDANCE

This culture of waste has also made us insensitive to wasting and throwing out excess foodstuffs, which is especially condemnable when, in every part of the world, unfortunately, many people and families suffer hunger and malnutrition. There was a time when our grandparents were very careful not to throw away any leftover food.

For today, reflect on the problem of the loss and waste of food. Consider contributing to a local food bank, volunteering at a soup kitchen, or donating to a cause that helps feed the hungry.

BECOME A LITTLE POORER

Poverty today is a cry. We must all think about whether we can become a little poorer. This is something we must all do. How I can become a little poorer to be more like Jesus, who was the poor Teacher. This is the thing.

For today, plan to sacrifice one thing in order to donate to someone less fortunate so that that person can have his or her basic needs met.

October **18**

SIGNS OF THE TIMES

My choices, including those related to the day-to-day aspects of life, like the use of a modest car, are related to a spiritual discernment that responds to a need that arises from looking at things, at people and from reading the signs of the times.

For today, ask: How can I live more simply so that I can focus on what's important in life? Consider whether it may be time to scale back your activities or your family's activities in order to make time for togetherness and prayer.

FOCUS ON THE POOR

If the investments in the banks fall slightly . . . a tragedy . . . But if people die of hunger, if they have nothing to eat, if they have poor health, it does not matter! This is our crisis today!

For today, pray that the world focus more of its attention and energies on resolving the tragedy of poverty and hunger. What can you do to alleviate these burdens? Invest some thought into answering this question, and if you already respond to the needs of the hungry, continue your good work.

October *20*

PRAY FOR CHILDREN

Unfortunately, what is thrown away is not only food and dispensable objects, but often human beings themselves, who are discarded as "unnecessary." For example, it is frightful even to think there are children, victims of abortion, who will never see the light of day; children being used as soldiers, abused and killed in armed conflicts; and children being bought and sold in that terrible form of modern slavery which is human trafficking, which is a crime against humanity.

For today, pray for the suffering children of the world, that they would be delivered from abuse, trafficking, and other bad situations and that their lives would be restored to the fullness God desires for them.

October *21*

USE YOUR TIME
TO PRAY

Today what counts as news is, maybe, a scandal. A scandal: ah, that is news! Today, the thought that a great many children do not have food to eat is not news. This is serious, this is serious! We cannot put up with this!

For today, avoid spending time reading about celebrity scandals as a form of entertainment. Instead, use those few minutes to pray for those who are hungry and suffering right now, that the Lord would guide their path and help them find the food they need.

BRING GOD'S CONSOLATION TO OTHERS

People today certainly need words, but most of all they need us to bear witness to the mercy and tenderness of the Lord, which warms the heart, rekindles hope, and attracts people toward the good. What a joy it is to bring God's consolation to others!

For today, bring the consolation of God's love to someone who you think needs it. Perhaps bring a meal to someone who is homebound and lonely—if you don't know of anyone, contact your local church to see if they know of anyone who could use a prepared meal.

LEARN ABOUT HUNGER

I ask everyone to reflect on the problem of the loss and waste of food, to identify ways and approaches which, by seriously dealing with this problem, convey solidarity and sharing with the underprivileged.

For today, educate yourself about hunger in the United States. What are the underlying causes? What challenges do the hungry face? How many people go without a meal in the United States each day? Understanding is one key to learning how to help.

FIGHT FOR
THE UNBORN

A mong the vulnerable for whom the Church wishes to care with particular love and concern are unborn children, the most defenseless and innocent among us. Nowadays efforts are made to deny them their human dignity and to do with them whatever one pleases, taking their lives and passing laws preventing anyone from standing in the way of this.

For today, investigate ways you can become involved in fighting abortion through your parish. Consider participating in the March for Life next January.

REMEMBER THE HOMELESS

Today we also have to say "thou shalt not" to an economy of exclusion and inequality. Such an economy kills. How can it be that it is not a news item when an elderly homeless person dies of exposure, but it is news when the stock market loses two points?

For today, remember that many homeless will be without shelter during the upcoming winter months. Donate gently used coats and blankets to a shelter. Consider organizing a drive in your church or school to collect blankets for the homeless.

DO YOUR PART FOR THE EARTH

The consequences of environmental changes . . . remind us of the gravity of neglect and inaction. The time to find global solutions is running out. We can find appropriate solutions only if we act together and in agreement.

For today, do your part to eliminate greenhouse gas emissions. Use less electricity, walk instead of driving, when possible, and recycle what you can.

GOD'S TENDERNESS

How much the world needs tenderness today! The patience of God, the closeness of God, the tenderness of God.

For today, make it a point to demonstrate God's tenderness through your actions. Hug your family and those close to you. Avoid harsh words.

BUILD A
BETTER FUTURE

Jesus said it many times: "Do not be afraid." . . . Do not be afraid, go forward, build bridges of peace, play on a team, and make the future better. Remember that the future is in your hands.

For today, consider ways you can encourage young people to not lose hope, to work together for the good of the future. Watch for opportunities to educate and motivate.

HUMAN UNDERSTANDING

Human self-understanding changes with time and so also human consciousness deepens. Let us think of when slavery was accepted or the death penalty was allowed without any problem. So we grow in the understanding of the truth.

For today, reflect on the ways people, as a whole, have grown in understanding of the truth. Thank God for the strides that have been made to overcome racism and other conditions, and pray God will continue to deepen our understanding and growth in the truth.

PRAY FOR
THE FRAGILE

The victims of this [throwaway] culture are precisely the weakest and most fragile human beings—the unborn, the poorest, the sick and elderly, the seriously handicapped, etc.—who are in danger of being "thrown away," expelled from a system that must be efficient at all costs.

For today, pray for the elderly, sick, and disabled, that they will receive necessary care and find comfort in the Lord's presence. Pray for the tender loving service of their caregivers.

LIVE JUSTLY

This is the first thing that God said to Abraham: Walk in my presence and live blamelessly. . . . Always journeying, in the presence of the Lord, in the light of the Lord, seeking to live with the blamelessness that God asked of Abraham in his promise.

For today, remember that Jesus is with you always. Act accordingly.

A DAY OF HOPE

Hope is a little like leaven that expands our souls. There are difficult moments in life, but with hope the soul goes forward and looks ahead to what awaits us. Today is a day of hope. Our brothers and sisters are in the presence of God and we shall also be there, through the pure grace of the Lord, if we walk along the way of Jesus.

For today, All Saints' Day, research a patron saint of importance to you— perhaps someone related to your profession or a special interest. Pray for his or her intercession on your behalf.

PRAYING FOR ALL SOULS

If today we remember our brothers and sisters who have gone before us in life and are in Heaven, it is because they have been washed in the blood of Christ. This is our hope: the hope of Christ's blood! It is a hope that does not disappoint. If we walk with the Lord in life, he will never disappoint us!

For today, remember all who have gone before us, especially your family members and close friends. Take comfort in your loving memories of them, and ask the Lord to bring them into his presence. Remember also the holy souls who may have been forgotten; pray that they may see the face of God.

CALLED TO SERVE

Every man and woman who assumes the responsibility of governing should ask themselves these two questions: Do I love my people, so that I may better serve them? And am I humble enough to hear the opinions of others so as to choose the best way of governing?

For today, pray for our elected officials and those who are soon to be elected, that they may be guided by wisdom and serve the best interests of our communities and our nation.

PRAY FOR THOSE WHO GOVERN

Let us pray for leaders . . . that they govern us well. That they bring our homeland, our nations, our world, forward, to achieve peace and the common good.

For today, pray that the Holy Spirit would guide citizens as they choose their political leaders so that the leaders who will best serve the common good would be chosen.

CARING LEADERS

I beg the Lord to grant us more politicians who are genuinely disturbed by the state of society, the people, the lives of the poor! It is vital that government leaders and financial leaders take heed and broaden their horizons, working to ensure that all citizens have dignified work, education and healthcare.

For today, read as much as you can about the beliefs of each of your newly elected political representatives. Plan to get involved by working for change if you disagree with something happening in your community.

PRAY FOR SINCERE AND CAPABLE LEADERS

I ask God to give us more politicians capable of sincere and effective dialogue aimed at healing the deepest roots—and not simply the appearances—of the evils in our world!

For today, pray that each candidate or newly elected government official takes time to self-reflect and to listen to the voices of his or her constituents.

APPEARANCES ARE FLEETING

So many Christians live for appearances
. . . their life seems like a soap bubble . . .
pretty, it's colorful, but it lasts for a second.

For today, resolve to spend more time
growing your heart and your understanding
of others and less time on managing your
outward appearance to others.

READY TO MEET GOD

All of us will experience sundown, all of us! Do we look at it with hope? Do we look with that joy at being welcomed by the Lord?

For today, at or near sunset, contemplate how you might feel when you approach the end of your days. Will you be ready to meet God? What can you do now to get ready?

GIVE SOMETHING

None of us can say, "I have nothing to do with this, they govern." . . . I have to do my best by participating in politics according to my ability. Politics, according to the Social Doctrine of the Church, is one of the highest forms of charity, because it serves the common good. I cannot wash my hands, eh? We all have to give something!

For today, refuse to wash your hands of the problems of the world. You need not be a politician to work for change.

RESPECT THE YOUTH

I have been closely following the news reports of the many young people who throughout the world have taken to the streets in order to express their desire for a more just and fraternal society. . . . It is the young who want to be the protagonists of change.

For today, resolve to recognize the work and optimism of today's youth. Be truthful and candid with those younger than you. Show them respect as you would your peers. Avoid condescension.

IN HONOR OF VETERANS DAY

Present generations should express their full recognition to all those who made such a heavy sacrifice. (Pope Francis's message commemorating the June 6, 1944, invasion of Normandy)

For today, pray for the veterans of all wars, that they may find the strength to overcome injuries and traumatic memories, and live in peace the remainder of their days. Pray for veterans who have died, that they may find solace in the arms of the Lord.

PRAY FOR AN END TO WAR

War is madness. It is the suicide of humanity. It is an act of faith in money, which for the mighty of this earth is more important than people.

For today, pray for the end to war and for an increased understanding among people of all nations.

REJECT THE CULT OF MONEY

The worship of the golden calf of old has found a new and heartless image in the cult of money and the dictatorship of an economy which is faceless and lacking any truly humane goal.

For today, consider how money can have power over people and cause us to behave in cruel ways. Vow to never let money rule in your life—give your heart to God alone. Always consider the plight of the poor.

CREATED TO DO GOOD

The root of this possibility of doing good—that we all have—is in creation. . . . The Lord created us in His image and likeness, and we are the image of the Lord, and He does good and all of us have this commandment at heart: do good and do not do evil.

For today, remember that God created us all to do good, regardless of our culture or inherited political or religious beliefs. Refrain from focusing on the differences and shortcomings of people, and instead focus on their potential to do good.

November **15**

STRIP YOURSELF OF WORLDLINESS

Someone could ask: Of what must the Church divest herself? Today she must strip herself of a very grave danger, which threatens every person in the Church, everyone: the danger of worldliness. The Christian cannot coexist with the spirit of the world, with the worldliness that leads us to vanity, to arrogance, to pride.

For today, be aware of times you may act prideful or arrogant toward others and resolve to strip yourself of those tendencies.

ETHICAL POLITICS

There is a need for financial reform along ethical lines that would produce in its turn an economic reform to benefit everyone. This would nevertheless require a courageous change of attitude on the part of political leaders.

Pray that our political leaders will find the courage to make policy decisions that are fair for all, including the most needy among us.

SAFEGUARD YOUR LIGHT

This mission of giving light to the world is so beautiful! We have this mission, and it is beautiful! It is also beautiful to keep the light we have received from Jesus, protecting it and safeguarding it.

For today, safeguard the light of Jesus within you—vow to never let the world quench that light. Entrust your cares to the Lord, and ask God to give you strength when your obstacles seem insurmountable.

DREAM OF HAPPY FAMILIES

I am very fond of dreams. . . . For nine months every mother and father dream about their baby. Am I right? [Yes!] They dream about what kind of child he or she will be. . . . You can't have a family without dreams. Once a family loses the ability to dream, children do not grow, love does not grow.

For today, allow the dreams of happy family life to guide you to show love and give love—to your children and spouse, if you are married. If you are single, through your kindness, reveal God's love to the people that the Lord has given you in your life: to parents, neighbors, friends, co-workers, acquaintances.

PRAY FOR SOCIAL WORKERS

When it comes to social issues, it is one thing to have a meeting to study the problem of drugs in a slum neighborhood and quite another thing to go there, live there and understand the problem from the inside and study it.

For today, pray for social workers and humanitarians who have the courage to go directly to the needy in order to more fully understand their situations and provide help.

BELOVED CHILDREN

A child is loved because he is one's child: not because he is beautiful, or because he is like this or like that; no, because he is a child! Not because he thinks as I do, or embodies my dreams. A child is a child: a life generated by us but intended for him, for his good, for the good of the family, of society, of mankind as a whole.

For today, pray for children, that they will have opportunities to love and be loved, to achieve their potential, and to fulfill God's plan for them.

IN THANKSGIVING

I f we can realize that everything is God's gift, how happy will our hearts be! Everything is his gift. He is our strength!

For today, as we approach the Thanksgiving holiday in the United States, give thanks to God for all you've received, and remember those who are less fortunate. Perhaps plan to volunteer at a shelter that provides Thanksgiving dinner for the homeless.

VIOLENCE IS NEVER THE ANSWER

At this moment in which we are praying intensely for peace, this word of the Lord touches us to the core, and essentially tells us: there is a more profound war that we must all fight! It is the firm and courageous decision to renounce evil and its enticements and to choose the good.

For today, pray for the conversion of those who use violence against others, that they would fight the evil that tempts their hearts.

November *23*

SAY THANK YOU

Saying "thank you" is such an easy thing, and yet so hard! How often do we say "thank you" to one another in our families? These are essential words for our life in common.

For today, remember to say a simple but sincere thanks to members of your family— not just for preparing a meal, caring for a child, or earning a wage, but for being a loving, present member of your family.

PRACTICE WHAT YOU TEACH

May we learn to say "thank you" to God and to one another. We teach children to do it, and then we forget to do it ourselves!

For today, say thank you to others outside your family—in your community, your church, or in your workplace.

A TREASURE FOR ALL

Priestly joy is a priceless treasure, not only for the priest himself but for the entire faithful people of God: that faithful people from which he is called to be anointed and which he, in turn, is sent to anoint. Anointed with the oil of gladness so as to anoint others with the oil of gladness.

For today, remember priests you have known who were joyful, who made you want to come to Mass. Pray that all who are called to the priesthood live it out with that magnitude of joy, to become treasures for the Church and all of the faithful.

DO NOT CAUSE SCANDAL

These sins of ours . . . it is right that they stir great sorrow in us, especially when we set a bad example and we notice we have to become a source of scandal. . . . Let us ask not be a source of scandal.

For today, refrain from judging those at the center of a public scandal; remember that it is the Lord who knows their hearts, not us. Also do some self-reflection, and consider the example you set for others. Repent if you realize that you may have caused others to sin because of the example you have given.

AN IMPORTANT ROLE

How often we forget to dedicate ourselves to that which truly matters! We forget that we are children of God.

For today, as you perform your roles as worker, friend, parent, grandparent, adult child, caregiver, or homeowner, remember your most important role of all—son or daughter of God.

THOSE WHO CAME BEFORE US

Our elders are men and women, fathers and mothers, who came before us on our own road, in our own house, in our daily battle for a worthy life. They are men and women from whom we have received so much.

For today, remember the elders in your life, and vow to spend as much time as possible with them—talking, listening, or sharing a meal. Enjoy your time with them, as their days may be short.

PRAY FOR AN END TO VIOLENCE AGAINST WOMEN

We cannot overlook the fact that wars involve another horrendous crime, the crime of rape. This is a most grave offense against the dignity of women, who are not only violated in body but also in spirit, resulting in a trauma hard to erase and with effects on society as well. Sadly, even apart from situations of war, all too many women even today are victims of violence.

For today, pray for all women who are victims of rape, domestic abuse, or sexual assault, that they may find healing and peace in the arms of our Savior; and for the abusers, that they may see the evil in their ways and seek forgiveness.

HUMBLE JOY

I can say that the most beautiful and natural expressions of joy which I have seen in my life were in poor people who had little to hold on to.

For today, remember when you've encountered someone who didn't seem to have many possessions and yet seemed content. Did you feel sorry for that person? Or did you wish you could be as content with so little? Vow to appreciate what you have and be thankful.

December 1

WORLD AIDS DAY

Today is the World Day for the battle against HIV/AIDS. We express our closeness to all people whom it has affected, especially children. This closeness is made concrete through the silent commitment of so many missionaries and workers. Let us pray for everyone . . . May every sick person, without exception, have access to the care they need.

For today, on World AIDS Day, consider one way you can help: Pray to the Holy Spirit for the success of those in the medical field looking for better treatments and a cure. Get informed about the issue. Contribute financially or volunteer for an AIDS hospice or nonprofit that cares for AIDS patients, such as Caritas Internationalis or the Missionaries of Charity.

December *2*

A GUIDE FOR ADVENT

From your great coastal cities to the plains of the Midwest, from the deep South to the far reaches of the West, wherever your people gather in the Eucharistic assembly, may the Pope be not simply a name but a felt presence, sustaining the fervent plea of the Bride: "Come, Lord!"

For today, as Advent begins and we await the coming of the Christ child, prepare your heart to receive the Lord. Listen closer to his Word. Remember, the Word of God, who came to us first in the littleness of a small child in Bethlehem, will come again in glory to fulfill all history. Let your heart always be ready for the coming of the Lord Jesus.

December *3*

THE PRINCIPLE OF GOD'S LOVE

Christians, in fact, go to meet the poor and the weak not to obey an ideological program, but because the word and the example of the Lord tell us that we are all brothers and sisters. This is the principle of God's love and of all justice among men.

For today, pray for your brothers and sisters who are suffering in some way, that they may find strength to overcome challenges. Donate to the giving tree at your church, or help to organize one if your church doesn't yet have one set up.

PATIENCE OF THE POOR

I see the holiness . . . in the patience of the people of God: a woman who is raising children, a man who works to bring home the bread, the sick, the elderly priests who have so many wounds but have a smile on their faces because they served the Lord, the sisters who work hard and live a hidden sanctity. This is for me the common sanctity.

For today, reflect on those who toil patiently, day after day, to care for their families, friends, and neighbors in the most bleak situations. Let them be an example of patience for you—never let your trust in God waver.

December *5*

WALK IN THE LIGHT

If we love God and our brothers and sisters, we walk in the light; but if our heart is closed, if we are dominated by pride, deceit, self-seeking, then darkness falls within us and around us.

For today, take joy in an open heart and your love for and from God. Greet everyone today with warm wishes. Take a small gift to someone who may be lonely this season.

BE AN ARTISAN OF PEACE

All of us want peace. Many people build it day by day through small gestures and acts; many of them are suffering, yet patiently persevere in their efforts to be peacemakers. All of us—especially those placed at the service of their respective peoples—have the duty to become instruments and artisans of peace, especially by our prayers.

For today, accept your duty as an artisan of peace. What role—large or small—can you play as a peacemaker in your home, workplace, or community?

GOD DREAMS WITH US

God does not dream by himself, he tries to do everything "with us." . . . The family is the living symbol of the loving plan of which the Father once dreamed. To want to form a family is to resolve to be a part of God's dream, to choose to dream with him, to want to build with him, to join him in this saga of building a world where no one will feel alone, unwanted or homeless.

For today, do something to build up your family or the great family of God—of which we all are a vital part. Let the Father's love for you inspire your love for others.

December 8

ON THE SOLEMNITY OF THE IMMACULATE CONCEPTION

On this Solemnity, then, by contemplating our beautiful Immaculate Mother, let us also recognize our truest destiny, our deepest vocation: to be loved, to be transformed by love, to be transformed by the beauty of God. . . . Let us allow ourselves to be watched over by her so that we may learn how to be more humble, and also more courageous in following the Word of God.

For today, on the Solemnity of the Immaculate Conception, thank God for his gift of our Immaculate Mother, Mary, and ask for her protection.

THE GIFT OF PARENTHOOD

Motherhood and fatherhood are a gift of God, but to accept the gift, to be astounded by its beauty and to make it shine in society, this is your task. Each of your children is a unique creature that will never be duplicated in the history of humanity.

For today, pray for all parents to recognize the unique gift that is each of their children.

JESUS IS OUR PEACE

Do not be afraid! Our Father is patient, he loves us, he gives us Jesus to guide us on the way which leads to the promised land. Jesus is the light who brightens the darkness. . . . He is our peace.

For today, put your troubles aside, and concentrate on following Jesus; trust him to help you find solutions and the strength to carry on.

BE PART OF JESUS' FAMILY

Doing God's will makes us become part of Jesus' family, it makes us his mother, father, sister, brother.

For today, meditate on what it means to be part of Jesus' family. He is always with you in good times and bad. Don't turn your back on him.

OUR LADY OF GUADALUPE

On this Feast of Our Lady of Guadalupe, let us first of all gratefully remember her visit and maternal closeness; let us sing her *Magnificat* with her; and let us entrust the life of our peoples and the continental mission of the Church to her.

For today, read and reflect on the Magnificat of Mary in Luke, chapter 1, verses 46-55, also called the Canticle of Mary. *Let her prayer of praise and exaltation of God become the prayer of your soul as well.*

13

MARY, QUEEN OF PEACE

Let us now invoke Mary, Queen of Peace. During her life on earth, she met many difficulties, related to the daily toils of life. But she never lost peace of heart, the fruit of faithful abandonment to God's mercy. Let us ask Mary, our gentle Mother, to show the entire world the sure way of love and peace.

For today, pray for the intercession of Mary, that peace will reign throughout this Advent season.

14

PRAY FOR
THE INNOCENT

How many innocent people and children suffer in the world! Lord, grant us your peace!

For today, pray for those who have lost children to violence, that faith in the Lord will heal their hearts and bring them peace.

GOD DOES NOT ABANDON US

I n the roughest moments, remember: God is our Father; God does not abandon his children.

For today, as hard as it may seem, put your life in God's hands instead of asking why. Trust the Lord when something bad happens, even when you don't have answers.

HORIZON OF HOPE

For the great human family it is always necessary to rediscover the common horizon toward which we are journeying. *The horizon of hope!* This is the horizon that makes for a good journey.

For today, pray for hope for all during the Advent journey of awaiting the Lord, for hope as we await the coming of peace, fulfillment, joy, and the fullness of love, which are his gift to us.

THE PATH TO CHRISTMAS

Saints always have joy in their faces. Or at least, amid suffering, a face of peace. The greatest suffering, the martyrdom of Jesus: He always had peace in his face and was concerned about others: his mother, John, the thief. . . . His concern was for others. . . . May Our Lady accompany us on this path toward Christmas. And let there be joy, joy!

For today, even as we approach the season of joy, the birth of Jesus, remember that there are still those among our family, friends, and community who suffer. Pray that they would have the gift of the Lord's peace and the loving accompaniment of Mary, our mother.

BE OPEN TO GOD'S CONSOLATION

In consolation the Holy Spirit is the protagonist! It is He who consoles us, it is He who gives us the courage to go out of ourselves. It is He who opens the door to the source of every true comfort, that is, the Father. And this is conversion. Please, let yourselves be comforted by the Lord!

For today, prepare for Jesus' coming by opening yourself to God's consolation so that you can be a source of consolation to others who maybe going through a difficult time.

GOD SURPRISES US

O*penness to being surprised by God.* Anyone who is a man or a woman of hope—the great hope which faith gives us—knows that even in the midst of difficulties, God acts and he surprises us. . . . He asks us to let ourselves be surprised by his love, to accept his surprises. Let us trust God!

For today, ponder a time you were surprised by God. Perhaps you didn't know what to do about a situation, and the answer suddenly occurred to you. Perhaps a prayer was answered quickly. Thank God for all the new ways in which he surprises us with his goodness.

MARY'S FAITH

Surely in her heart she said to the baby she was carrying in her womb: "Come, I want to see your face, for they have told me you will be great!"

For today, meditate on the birth story of Jesus, and if possible, tell the story to a child in your life, or read them an age-appropriate book. Join in Mary's anticipation!

VULNERABLE INFANT JESUS

We bless you, Lord God most high, who lowered yourself for our sake. You are immense, and you made yourself small; you are rich and you made yourself poor; you are all-powerful and you made yourself vulnerable.

For today, as we anxiously await Christmas, say a prayer of gratitude to God for sending us his Son.

THE REASON FOR CHRISTMAS

Ensure that Holy Christmas is never a celebration of commercial consumerism, of appearances or of useless gifts, or of excessive waste, but that it is a celebration of joyfully welcoming the Lord into the crib and into the heart.

For today, as hard as it is to not get caught up in the holiday rush, set aside time to read Scripture surrounding Jesus' imminent birth. Stress the reason for the season with the children or young people in your life.

CHRISTIAN JOY

Christian joy, like hope, is founded on God's fidelity, on the certainty that he always keeps his promises.

For today, as Christmas draws closer, contemplate Christian joy—the joy we feel in anticipation of the Lord's coming. Find ways to express that joy with your family, through singing carols or volunteering together for a cause.

A GREAT LIGHT

This is how the liturgy of this holy Christmas night presents to us the birth of the Savior: as the light which pierces and dispels the deepest darkness. The presence of the Lord in the midst of his people cancels the sorrow of defeat and the misery of slavery, and ushers in joy and happiness.

For today, set aside some quiet time to reflect on how God has shattered the darkness of sin. If possible, attend the Christmas Vigil tonight to commemorate the birth of the Light of the World.

December *25*

A SAVIOR IS BORN

Jesus, the Son of God, the Savior of the world, is born for us, born in Bethlehem of a Virgin, fulfilling the ancient prophecies.

For today, after all of the presents have been unwrapped, reflect with your family, friends, and loved ones on God's gift of a divine Savior for us. Say a prayer of thanksgiving for this eternal gift of our heavenly Father.

WELCOMING THE INFANT JESUS

While we contemplate the Infant Jesus just born and placed in the manger, we are invited to reflect. How do we welcome the tenderness of God? Do I allow myself to be taken up by God, to be embraced by him, or do I prevent him from drawing close? . . . The question put to us simply by the Infant's presence is: do I allow God to love me?

For today, when advertisements for after-Christmas sales are everywhere, don't forget that the Christmas celebration continues until the Feast of the Baptism of the Lord (in January). Celebrate God who humbled himself in the smallness of a baby. Reflect on these questions: How will you welcome the Infant Jesus? Will you receive his love for you?

December *27*

GOD'S CREATION

Every creature is the object of the Father's tenderness, who gives it its place in the world.

For today, appreciate the beauty of knowing that God's tenderness covers all creation, including all humanity, all the creatures of the earth, and all natural wonders. Give thanks for the diversity of peoples and the magnificence of our natural world.

JESUS, OUR SALVATION

Yes, brothers and sisters, Jesus is the salvation for every person and for every people!

For today, rejoice in the miracle of Jesus' birth, through which God came to be among us, to save us and every person from sin, darkness, and death!

A MESSAGE OF HOPE

Dear brothers and sisters, may the Holy Spirit today enlighten our hearts, that we may recognize in the Infant Jesus, born in Bethlehem of the Virgin Mary, the salvation given by God to each one of us, to each man and woman and to all the peoples of the earth.

For today, as the excitement of the Christmas holidays winds down and life returns to a calmer pace, carry the hope of the newborn Savior in your heart. Spread this message of hope and Christmas joy to those you encounter.

A CHANNEL OF GOD'S PEACE

G od is peace: let us ask him to help us to be peacemakers each day, in our life, in our families, in our cities and nations, in the whole world. Let us allow ourselves to be moved by God's goodness.

For today, as you begin preparations for the new year, vow to keep the hope of Christ alive in your heart. Try to promote peace within your family and community and everywhere you can. Pray for those who are alone or suffering this Christmas.

NURTURE THE LIGHT

Like Mary, may we nurture the light born within us at Christmas. May we carry it everywhere in our daily lives.

For today, pray for peace in the coming year so that you may faithfully do God's work, carrying the living light of Christ and sharing it with others.

Notes

JANUARY

January 1
Address at Meeting with Personnel of the Holy See and Vatican City State. Paul VI Audience Hall. December 22, 2014.

January 2
Address on Vigil of Pentecost to Ecclesial Movements. St. Peter's Square. May 18, 2013.

January 3
Encyclical Letter *The Light of Faith* (*Lumen Fidei*). June 29, 2013.

January 4
Angelus. St. Peter's Square. February 16, 2014.

January 5
Morning Meditation. Chapel of the *Domus Sanctae Marthae*. May 10, 2013. Vatican Radio translation.

January 6
Homily at Holy Mass for "Evangelium Vitae" Day. St. Peter's Square. June 16, 2013.

January 7
General Audience. St. Peter's Square. June 12, 2013.

January 8
Morning Meditation. Chapel of the *Domus Sanctae Marthae*.
January 9, 2014. *L'Osservatore Romano* translation.

January 9
Morning Meditation. Chapel of the *Domus Sanctae Marthae*.
January 9, 2014. *L'Osservatore Romano* translation.

January 10
Morning Meditation. Chapel of the *Domus Sanctae Marthae*.
January 10, 2014. Vatican Radio translation.

January 11
Twitter post (Pontifex). January 17, 2017, 8:30 p.m.

January 12
Address at Meeting with Personnel of the Holy See and Vatican
City State. Paul VI Audience Hall. December 22, 2014.

January 13
Morning Meditation. Chapel of the *Domus Sanctae Marthae*.
January 13, 2014. *L'Osservatore Romano* translation.

January 14
Address at Meeting with Personnel of the Holy See and Vatican
City State. Paul VI Audience Hall. December 22, 2014.

January 15
Message on the Occasion of the "Mexico/Holy See Colloquium on
Migration and Development. Mexico City. July 14, 2014.

January 16
Twitter post (Pontifex). November 18, 2014, 2:18 a.m.

January 17

Address at Meeting with Personnel of the Holy See and Vatican City State. Paul VI Audience Hall. December 22, 2014.

January 18

General Audience. St. Peter's Square. May 1, 2013.

January 19

Morning Meditation. Chapel of the *Domus Sanctae Marthae*. January 9, 2015.

January 20

Morning Meditation. Chapel of the *Domus Sanctae Marthae*. January 21, 2014.

January 21

Morning Meditation. Chapel of the *Domus Sanctae Marthae*. January 20, 2014.

January 22

Address at Meeting with the Members of the UN General Assembly on Apostolic Journey to Cuba and the United States of America (September 19-28). UN Headquarters, New York. September 25, 2015.

January 23

Morning Meditation. Chapel of the *Domus Sanctae Marthae*. January 28, 2014.

January 24

Message for the Forty-Eighth World Communications Day (June 1, 2014). Given on January 24, 2014.

January 25
Interview by Fr. Antonio Spadaro, Editor-in-Chief of the Italian Jesuit Magazine *La Civiltà Cattolica*. Rome. August 19, 23, and 29, 2013.

January 26
Twitter post (Pontifex). April 28, 2015, 1:28 a.m.

January 27
Twitter post (Pontifex). January 27, 2015, 3:00 a.m.

January 28
Address on Pilgrimage to the Holy Land. Yad Vashem Memorial, Jerusalem. May 26, 2014.

January 29
Homily at Easter Vigil. Vatican Basilica. March 30, 2013.

January 30
General Audience. St. Peter's Square. May 15, 2013.

January 31
Twitter post (Pontifex). March 5, 2015, 12:30 a.m.

FEBRUARY

February 1
Twitter post (Pontifex). April 28, 2014, 1:28 a.m.

February 2
Homily on the Occasion of the Eighteenth World Day of Consecrated Life. Vatican Basilica. February 2, 2014.

February 3
Homily at Mass for the Possession of the Chair of the Bishop of Rome. Basilica of St. John Lateran. April 7, 2013.

February 4
Twitter post (Pontifex). June 2, 2013, 3:12 a.m.

February 5
Homily at Mass for the Possession of the Chair of the Bishop of Rome. Basilica of St. John Lateran. April 7, 2013.

February 6
Morning Meditation. Chapel of the *Domus Sanctae Marthae*. February 6, 2014.

February 7
Homily at Holy Mass. Basilica of St. Paul Outside the Walls. April 14, 2013.

February 8
Press Conference. Return Flight from Strasbourg to Rome after his visit to the European Parliament and to the Council of Europe. November 25, 2014.

February 9
Twitter post (Pontifex). August 23, 2014, 1:23 a.m.

February 10
Twitter post (Pontifex). August 19, 2013, 3:15 a.m.

February 11
Message for the Twenty-Third World Day of the Sick (Feb 11, 2015). Given December 3, 2014.

February 12
Twitter post (Pontifex). May 26, 2013, 3:26 a.m.

February 13
Twitter post (Pontifex). March 9, 2015, 4:00 a.m.

February 14
Address to Engaged Couples Preparing for Marriage. St. Peter's Square. February 14, 2014.

February 15
Address to Engaged Couples Preparing for Marriage. St. Peter's Square. February 14, 2014.

February 16
Homily at Holy Mass on the Occasion of the Year of Faith. St. Peter's Square. October 27, 2013.

February 17
Twitter post (Pontifex). April 29, 2013, 1:29 a.m.

February 18
Interview by Fr. Antonio Spadaro, Editor-in-Chief of the Italian Jesuit Magazine *La Civiltà Cattolica*. Rome. August 19, 23, and 29, 2013.

February 19
Urbi et Orbi Apostolic Blessing upon Election as Pope. St. Peter's Square. March 13, 2013.

February 20
Morning Meditation. Chapel of the *Domus Sanctae Marthae*. January 23, 2014.

February 21
General Audience. St. Peter's Square. June 5, 2013.

February 22
Address at Way of the Cross with Young People on the Occasion of the Twenty-Eighth World Youth Day. Waterfront of Copacabana, Rio de Janeiro. July 26, 2013.

February 23
Twitter post (Pontifex). February 6, 2015, 12:06 a.m.

February 24
Twitter post (Pontifex). August 5, 2013, 3:05 a.m.

February 25
Twitter post (Pontifex). September 9, 2013, 2:12 a.m.

February 26
Homily at Mass for the Beginning of the Petrine Ministry of the Bishop of Rome. St. Peter's Square. March 19, 2013.

February 27
Morning Meditation. Chapel of the *Domus Sanctae Marthae*. February 27, 2014

February 28
Homily at Holy Mass with Blessing and Imposition of Ashes. Basilica of Santa Sabina. February 18, 2015.

February 29
Homily at Holy Mass on the Occasion of the Year of Faith. St. Peter's Square. October 27, 2013.

MARCH

March 1
Press Conference. Return Flight from Rio de Janeiro on the
Occasion of the Twenty-Eighth World Youth Day. July 28, 2013.

March 2
Address to Participants in the Plenary Assembly of the Pontifical
Council for Culture. Consistory Hall. February 7, 2015.

March 3
Twitter post (Pontifex). September 25, 2013, 11:26 a.m.

March 4
Message for Lent 2015. Given October 4, 2014.

March 5
Twitter post (Pontifex). July 27, 2013, 6:27 p.m.

March 6
General Audience. St. Peter's Square. June 11, 2014.

March 7
Homily at Holy Mass and Canonization of Blessed Fr. Junípero
Serra on Apostolic Journey to Cuba and the United States of
America (September 19-28). National Shrine of the Immaculate
Conception, Washington, DC. September 23, 2015.

March 8
Interview by Fr. Antonio Spadaro, Editor-in-Chief of the Italian
Jesuit Magazine *La Civiltà Cattolica*. Rome. August 19, 23,
and 29, 2013.

March 9
Interview by Fr. Antonio Spadaro, Editor-in-Chief of the Italian Jesuit Magazine *La Civiltà Cattolica*. Rome. August 19, 23, and 29, 2013.

March 10
Twitter post (Pontifex). March 31, 2014, 2:00 a.m.

March 11
Message for Lent 2014. Given December 26, 2013.

March 12
Phone Call to Participants in Thirty-Sixth Annual Walking Pilgrimage from Macerata to Loreto. June 7, 2014.

March 13
Twitter post (Pontifex). February 17, 2015, 1:00 a.m.

March 14
Message for Lent 2014. Given December 26, 2013.

March 15
Twitter post (Pontifex). May 16, 2015, 1:45 a.m.

March 16
Message for Lent 2014. Given December 26, 2013.

March 17
Angelus. St. Peter's Square. March 17, 2013.

March 18
Morning Meditation. Chapel of the *Domus Sanctae Marthae*. February 17, 2014. *L'Osservatore Romano* translation.

March 19
General Audience. St. Peter's Square. March 19, 2014.

March 20
Address to the New Non-Resident Ambassadors to the Holy See. Clementine Hall. May 16, 2013.

March 21
General Audience. St. Peter's Square. April 3, 2013.

March 22
Letter to the Italian Journalist Dr. Eugenio Scalfari. September 4, 2013.

March 23
Morning Meditation in the Chapel of the *Domus Sanctae Marthae*. December 15, 2014.

March 24
Message for Lent 2014. Given December 26, 2013.

March 25
Homily at Holy Mass and Conferral of the Sacrament of Confirmation. St. Peter's Square. April 28, 2013.

March 26
Homily at Mass for the Beginning of the Petrine Ministry of the Bishop of Rome. St. Peter's Square. March 19, 2013.

March 27
Homily at Celebration of Vespers on the Conversion of St. Paul the Apostle. Basilica of St. Paul Outside the Walls. January 25, 2015.

March 28
Twitter post (Pontifex). May 12, 2015, 1:12 a.m.

March 29
Twitter post (Pontifex). June 30, 2015, 1:30 a.m.

March 30
Apostolic Exhortation *The Joy of the Gospel* (*Evangelii Gaudium*), no. 131. November 24, 2013.

March 31
Homily at Celebration of Palm Sunday of the Passion of our Lord. St. Peter's Square. March 24, 2014.

APRIL

April 1
Angelus. St. Peter's Square. March 17, 2013.

April 2
Twitter post (Pontifex). January 10, 2015, 1:00 a.m.

April 3
Press Conference on Flight from Colombo to Manila. Apostolic Journey to Sri Lanka and the Philippines. January 15, 2015.

April 4
Angelus. St. Peter's Square. June 23, 2013.

April 5
Morning Meditation. Chapel of the *Domus Sanctae Marthae*. Friday February 20, 2015.

April 6
Message for Lent 2014. Given December 26, 2013.

April 7
Twitter post (Pontifex). April 12, 2014, 3:00 a.m.

April 8
Morning Meditation. Chapel of the *Domus Sanctae Marthae*.
September 16, 2013. Vatican Radio translation.

April 9
Homily at Holy Mass. Basilica of St. Paul Outside the Walls.
April 14, 2013.

April 10
General Audience. St. Peter's Square. April 3, 2013.

April 11
Message for Fifty-First World Day of Prayer for Vocations.
May 11, 2014.

April 12
General Audience. St. Peter's Square. May 1, 2013.

April 13
General Audience. St. Peter's Square. February 18, 2015.

April 14
Address to the New Non-Resident Ambassadors to the Holy See.
Clementine Hall. May 16, 2013.

April 15
Twitter post (Pontifex). May 23, 2014, 3:00 a.m.

April 16
Homily at Vigil of Prayer for Peace. St. Peter's Square.
September 7, 2013.

April 17
Homily at Mass for the Beginning of the Petrine Ministry of the
Bishop of Rome. St. Peter's Square. March 19, 2013.

April 18
Encyclical Letter *Laudato Si'*, no. 92. May 24, 2015.

April 19
Twitter post (Pontifex). August 9, 2014, 10:00 a.m.

April 20
Message for the World Day of Peace (January 1, 2014). Given December 8, 2013.

April 21
Address at the Plenary Session of the Pontifical Academy of Sciences. Casina of Pius IV. October 27, 2014.

April 22
Encyclical Letter *Laudato Si'*, no. 139. May 24, 2015.

April 23
Twitter post (Pontifex). December 11, 2014, 2:00 a.m.

April 24
General Audience. St. Peter's Square. May 21, 2014.

April 25
General Audience. St. Peter's Square. June 5, 2013.

April 26
General Audience. St. Peter's Square. June 26, 2013. Vatican Radio translation.

April 27
Address at the Plenary Session of the Pontifical Academy of Sciences. Casina of Pius IV. October 27, 2014.

April 28
Address at the Plenary Session of the Pontifical Academy of Sciences. Casina of Pius IV. October 27, 2014.

April 29
Urbi et Orbi Message. Easter Sunday, March 31, 2013.

April 30
Homily at Holy Mass on Apostolic Journey to Sri Lanka and the Philippines (January 12-19, 2015). Tacloban International Airport. January 17, 2015.

MAY

May 1
General Audience. St. Peter's Square. May 1, 2013.

May 2
General Audience. Paul VI Audience Hall. January 7, 2015.

May 3
General Audience. Paul VI Audience Hall. January 7, 2015.

May 4
Message for the Forty-Eighth World Communications Day (June 1, 2014). Given January 24, 2014.

May 5
Homily at Mass for the Beginning of the Petrine Ministry of the Bishop of Rome. St. Peter's Square. March 19, 2013.

May 6
Homily at Easter Vigil. Vatican Basilica. March 30, 2013.

May 7

General Audience. St. Peter's Square. September 10, 2014.

May 8

Morning Meditation. Chapel of the *Domus Sanctae Marthae*. February 20, 2015.

May 9

Address to Students and Teachers. St. Damasus Courtyard in the Vatican. August 21, 2013.

May 10

Message for the Twenty-Third World Day of the Sick (Feb 11, 2015). Given December 3, 2014.

May 11

General Audience. St. Peter's Square. June 4, 2014.

May 12

Homily at Holy Mass. Basilica of St. Paul Outside the Walls. April 14, 2013.

May 13

Message for the Twenty-Third World Day of the Sick (Feb 11, 2015). Given December 3, 2014.

May 14

Angelus. St. Peter's Square. February 22, 2015.

May 15

Twitter post (Pontifex). June 17, 2013, 1:17 a.m.

May 16

Message for the Thirtieth World Youth Day. January 31, 2015.

May 17

Twitter post (Pontifex). November 19, 2013, 6:19 a.m.

May 18

Message for the Twenty-Third World Day of the Sick (Feb 11, 2015). Given December 3, 2014.

May 19

Letter Concerning the Pontifical Commission for the Protection of Minors. February 2, 2015.

May 20

General Audience. St. Peter's Square. September 3, 2014. *L'Osservatore Romano* translation.

May 21

Address to Participants in the Plenary Assembly of the Pontifical Council for the Family. Clementine Hall. October 25, 2013.

May 22

Angelus. St. Peter's Square. June 23, 2013.

May 23

Message for the Twenty-Ninth World Youth Day. January 21, 2014.

May 24

Address at Meeting with the Poor Assisted by Caritas. Assisi. October 4, 2013.

May 25

Letter to the Italian Journalist Dr. Eugenio Scalfari. September 4, 2013.

May 26

Address at the Way of the Cross at the Colosseum. Palatine Hill. March 29, 2013.

May 27
General Audience. St. Peter's Square. May 8, 2013.

May 28
Regina Caeli on Divine Mercy Sunday. St. Peter's Square. April 7, 2013.

May 29
Morning Meditation. Chapel of the *Domus Sanctae Marthae*. September 25, 2014. Vatican Radio translation.

May 30
Message for the Thirtieth World Youth Day. January 31, 2015.

May 31
Message for the Thirtieth World Youth Day. January 31, 2015.

JUNE

June 1
Address to Participants in the Ecclesial Convention of the Diocese of Rome. Paul VI Audience Hall. June 17, 2013.

June 2
Homily at Holy Mass and Conferral of the Sacrament of Confirmation. St. Peter's Square. April, 28, 2013.

June 3
Message for the Forty-Eighth World Communications Day. June 1, 2014.

June 4
Morning Meditation. Chapel of the *Domus Sanctae Marthae*. January 23, 2015. Vatican Radio translation.

June 5
Interview by Fr. Antonio Spadaro, Editor-in-Chief of the Italian Jesuit Magazine *La Civiltà Cattolica*. Rome. August 19, 23, and 29, 2013.

June 6
Message for the Twenty-Ninth World Youth Day. January 21, 2014.

June 7
Address to Participants in the Pilgrimage of Catechists. Paul VI Audience Hall. September 27, 2013.

June 8
Address at Recital of the Holy Rosary. Papal Basilica of St. Mary Major. May 4, 2013.

June 9
Twitter post (Pontifex). March 4, 2014, 1:04 a.m.

June 10
Homily at Holy Mass. Basilica of St. Paul Outside the Walls. April 14, 2013.

June 11
Homily at Holy Mass. St. Peter's Square. October 13, 2013.

June 12
Homily at Holy Mass. St. Peter's Square. October 13, 2013.

June 13
Homily at Holy Mass. Basilica of St. Paul Outside the Walls. April 14, 2013.

June 14
Homily at Vigil of Prayer for Peace. St. Peter's Square. September 7, 2013.

June 15
General Audience. Paul VI Audience Hall. February 4, 2015.

June 16
Twitter post (Pontifex). January 16, 2015, 4:00 a.m.

June 17
Twitter post (Pontifex). April 3, 2014, 1:03 a.m.

June 18
Twitter post (Pontifex). July 31, 2014, 1:31 a.m.

June 19
Address at Meeting with Personnel of the Holy See and Vatican City State. Paul VI Audience Hall. December 22, 2014.

June 20
Address to Joint Session of the US Congress on Apostolic Journey to Cuba and the United States of America (September 19-28). US Capitol, Washington, DC. September 24, 2015.

June 21
Twitter post (Pontifex). March 12, 2015, 3:30 a.m.

June 22
Message for the Forty-Eighth World Communications Day (Sunday June 1, 2014). Given on January 24, 2014.

June 23
Homily at the Mass of the Lord's Supper. "Casal del Marmo" Prison for Minors, Rome. March 28, 2013.

June 24
Message for the Twenty-Ninth World Youth Day. January 21, 2014.

June 25
Press Conference. Return Flight from Rio de Janeiro on the
Occasion of the Twenty-Eighth World Youth Day. July 28, 2013.

June 26
General Audience. St. Peter's Square. March 11, 2015.

June 27
Message for the Twenty-Ninth World Youth Day. January 21, 2014.

June 28
General Audience. St. Peter's Square. April 17, 2013.

June 29
Twitter post (Pontifex). November 21, 2013, 6:21 a.m.

June 30
General Audience. St. Peter's Square. October 15, 2014.

JULY

July 1
Angelus. St. Peter's Square. June 30, 2013.

July 2
Interview by Fr. Antonio Spadaro, Editor-in-Chief of the Italian
Jesuit Magazine *La Civiltà Cattolica*. Rome. August 19, 23,
and 29, 2013.

July 3
Encyclical Letter *Laudato Si'* no. 237. May 24, 2015.

July 4
Morning Meditation. Chapel of the *Domus Sanctae Marthae*.
July 4, 2013.

July 5
Speech on the Occasion of the Twenty-Eighth World Youth Day. Prayer Vigil with Young People, Waterfront of Copacabana, Rio de Janeiro. July 27, 2013.

July 6
Address to the Students of the Jesuit Schools of Italy and Albania. Paul VI Audience Hall. June 7, 2013.

July 7
Twitter post (Pontifex). July 29, 2014, 2:29 a.m.

July 8
Message for the Twenty-Ninth World Youth Day. January 21, 2014.

July 9
Message for the Twenty-Ninth World Youth Day. January 21, 2014.

July 10
Twitter post (Pontifex). October 28, 2013, 7:15 a.m.

July 11
Twitter post (Pontifex). February 21, 2015, 2:30 a.m.

July 12
Apostolic Exhortation *The Joy of the Gospel* (*Evangelii Gaudium*), no. 97. November 24, 2013.

July 13
Angelus. St. Peter's Square. October 5, 2014.

July 14
Address to Participants in the Pilgrimage of Families. St. Peter's Square. October 26, 2013.

July 15
Address to Participants in the Pilgrimage of Families. St. Peter's Square. October 26, 2013.

July 16
Address to Participants in the Pilgrimage of Families. St. Peter's Square. October 26, 2013.

July 17
Morning Meditation. Chapel of the *Domus Sanctae Marthae*. October 31, 2014.

July 18
Address to Participants in the Pilgrimage of Families. St. Peter's Square. October 26, 2013.

July 19
Angelus. St. Peter's Square. March 17, 2013.

July 20
Address at Meeting with the Personnel of the Holy See and Vatican City State. Paul VI Audience Hall. December 22, 2014.

July 21
Interview by Fr. Antonio Spadaro, Editor-in-Chief of the Italian Jesuit Magazine *La Civiltà Cattolica*. Rome. August 19, 23, and 29, 2013.

July 22
Message for the Thirtieth World Youth Day. January 31, 2015.

July 23
Homily at Holy Mass on the Occasion of the Twenty-Eighth World Youth Day. Basilica of the Shrine of Our Lady of the Conception of Aparecida. July 24, 2013.

July 24

Interview by Fr. Antonio Spadaro, Editor-in-Chief of the Italian Jesuit Magazine *La Civiltà Cattolica*. Rome. August 19, 23, and 29, 2013.

July 25

General Audience. Paul VI Audience Hall. January 7, 2015.

July 26

Address to the National Numerous Family Association. Paul VI Hall. December 28, 2014.

July 27

Address to Engaged Couples Preparing for Marriage. St. Peter's Square. February 14, 2014.

July 28

Apostolic Exhortation *The Joy of the Gospel* (*Evangelii Gaudium*), no. 47. November 24, 2013.

July 29

Address at Meeting with Personnel of the Holy See and Vatican City State. Paul VI Audience Hall. December 22, 2014.

July 30

Twitter post (Pontifex). June 18, 2015, 1:00 p.m.

July 31

Address at Meeting with the Authorities During Apostolic Journey to the Republic of Korea. Chungmu Hall at the "Blue House" in Seoul. August 14, 2014.

AUGUST

August 1
Homily at *Missa Pro Ecclesia* with the Cardinal Electors. Sistine Chapel. March 14, 2013.

August 2
Homily at Chrism Mass on Holy Thursday. St. Peter's Basilica. March 28, 2013.

August 3
Twitter post (Pontifex). June 5, 2014, 2:05 a.m.

August 4
Angelus. St. Peter's Square. March 17, 2013.

August 5
Interview by Fr. Antonio Spadaro, Editor-in-Chief of the Italian Jesuit Magazine *La Civiltà Cattolica*. Rome. August 19, 23, and 29, 2013.

August 6
Angelus. St. Peter's Square. December 1, 2013.

August 7
Interview by Fr. Antonio Spadaro, Editor-in-Chief of the Italian Jesuit Magazine *La Civiltà Cattolica*. Rome. August 19, 23, and 29, 2013.

August 8
General Audience. St. Peter's Square. March 27, 2013. Vatican Radio translation.

August 9
Twitter post (Pontifex). March 24, 2013, 5:15 a.m.

August 10
Twitter post (Pontifex). September 18, 2014, 2:30 a.m.

August 11
Homily at Celebration of Palm Sunday of the Passion of Our Lord.
St. Peter's Square. March 24, 2013.

August 12
General Audience. St. Peter's Square. April 2, 2014.

August 13
Angelus. St. Peter's Square. October 26, 2014.

August 14
Homily at Celebration of Palm Sunday of the Passion of Our Lord.
St. Peter's Square. March 24, 2013.

August 15
Angelus on the Solemnity of the Assumption of the Blessed Virgin
Mary. Castel Gandolfo. August 15, 2013.

August 16
Address to the National Pilgrimage of German Altar Servers.
August 5, 2014.

August 17
Homily at Closing Mass of the Extraordinary Synod on the Family
and Beatification of the Servant of God Paul VI. St. Peter's Square.
October 19, 2014.

August 18
Homily at Mass for the Beginning of the Petrine Ministry of the
Bishop of Rome. St. Peter's Square. March 19, 2013.

August 19
Address at Meeting with the Elderly. St. Peter's Square.
September 28, 2014.

August 20
Interview by Fr. Antonio Spadaro, Editor-in-Chief of the Italian
Jesuit Magazine *La Civiltà Cattolica*. Rome. August 19, 23,
and 29, 2013.

August 21
Urbi et Orbi Message. Easter Sunday, March 31, 2013.

August 22
Twitter post (Pontifex). October 18, 2014, 4:15 a.m.

August 23
Address on Vigil of Pentecost to Ecclesial Movements. St. Peter's
Square. May 18, 2013.

August 24
Twitter post (Pontifex). February 3, 2014, 2:03 a.m.

August 25
Address to Representatives of the Communications Media. Paul VI
Audience Hall. March 16, 2013.

August 26
Twitter post (Pontifex). January 30, 2014, 3:30 a.m.

August 27
Twitter post (Pontifex). January 27, 2014, 1:27 a.m.

August 28
Morning Meditation. Chapel of the *Domus Sanctae Marthae*.
February 9, 2015.

August 29
Regina Caeli During Pilgrimage to the Holy Land. Bethlehem.
May 25, 2014.

August 30
Morning Meditation. Chapel of the *Domus Sanctae Marthae*.
January 26, 2015.

August 31
Twitter post (Pontifex). June 3, 2014, 3:00 a.m.

SEPTEMBER

September 1
Address on the Occasion of the Twenty-Eighth World Youth
Day. Welcome Ceremony at Garden of Guanabara Palace, Rio de
Janeiro. July 22, 2013.

September 2
Address at Meeting with Personnel of the Holy See and Vatican
City State. Paul VI Audience Hall. December 22, 2014.

September 3
Twitter post (Pontifex). June 2, 2014, 2:15 a.m.

September 4
Address at Meeting with Workers on Pastoral Visit to Cagliari.
Largo Carlo Felice, Cagliari. September 22, 2013.

September 5
Morning Meditation. Chapel of the *Domus Sanctae Marthae*.
February 20, 2015.

September 6
Message for the Forty-Ninth World Communications Day. Given on January 23, 2015.

September 7
Interview by Fr. Antonio Spadaro, Editor-in-Chief of the Italian Jesuit Magazine *La Civiltà Cattolica*. Rome. August 19, 23, and 29, 2013.

September 8
Message to the President of the Cuban Episcopal Conference on the Nativity of the Blessed Virgin Mary. September 8, 2014.

September 9
Morning Meditation. Chapel of the *Domus Sanctae Marthae*. January 26, 2015.

September 10
Bull of Indiction of the Extraordinary Jubilee of Mercy, *Misericordiae Vultus*. April 11, 2015.

September 11
Address at Interreligious Meeting on Apostolic Journey to Cuba and the United States of America (September 19-28). Ground Zero Memorial, New York. September 25, 2015.

September 12
Morning Meditation. Chapel of the *Domus Sanctae Marthae*. May 22, 2013.

September 13
Angelus. St. Peter's Square. October 5, 2014. Vatican Radio translation.

September 14

Address to the President of the Diyanet at the Department for Religious Affairs. Apostolic Journey to Ankara, Turkey. November 28, 2014.

September 15

Twitter post (Pontifex). August 23, 2013, 3:03 a.m.

September 16

Address to the Participants in the Plenary Assembly of the Pontifical Council for the Family. Clementine Hall. October 25, 2013.

September 17

Twitter post (Pontifex). June 17, 2014, 3:17 a.m.

September 18

Address to Participants in the Pilgrimage of Families. St. Peter's Square. October 26, 2013.

September 19

Message to the Vicar General for the Diocese of Rome. July 19, 2013.

September 20

Morning Meditation. Chapel of the *Domus Sanctae Marthae*. February 20, 2015.

September 21

Angelus. St. Peter's Square. January 4, 2015.

September 22

Twitter post (Pontifex). October 7, 2014, 4:00 a.m.

September 23
Address and Presentation of Christmas Greetings to the Roman Curia. Clementine Hall. December 22, 2014.

September 24
Address at Meeting with Personnel of the Holy See and Vatican City State. Paul VI Audience Hall. December 22, 2014.

September 25
Address to Participants in the Pilgrimage of Families. St. Peter's Square. October 26, 2013.

September 26
Address to Participants in the Pilgrimage of Families. St. Peter's Square. October 26, 2013.

September 27
Address to Participants in the Pilgrimage of Families. St. Peter's Square. October 26, 2013.

September 28
Address to Engaged Couples Preparing for Marriage. St. Peter's Square. February 14, 2014.

September 29
Message for the Forty-Ninth World Communications Day. Given on January 23, 2015.

September 30
Homily at Holy Mass for Family Day. St. Peter's Square. October 27, 2013.

OCTOBER

October 1
Address at Meeting Organized by the International Federation of Catholic Medical Associations. Clementine Hall. September 20, 2013.

October 2
Address at Meeting Organized by the International Federation of Catholic Medical Associations. Clementine Hall. September 20, 2013.

October 3
Message to Catholics in Ireland, Scotland, England and Wales. July 17, 2013. Vatican Radio.

October 4
Address to Representatives of the Communications Media. Paul VI Audience Hall. March 16, 2013.

October 5
Address to the Participants in the World Meeting of Popular Movements. Old Synod Hall. October 28, 2014.

October 6
Interview by Fr. Antonio Spadaro, Editor-in-Chief of the Italian Jesuit Magazine *La Civiltà Cattolica*. Rome. August 19, 23, and 29, 2013.

October 7
Homily at Holy Mass on Apostolic Journey to Sri Lanka and the Philippines (January 12-19, 2015). Rizal Park, Manila. January 18, 2015.

October 8
Address to the Students of the Jesuit Schools of Italy and Albania.
Paul VI Audience Hall. June 7, 2013.

October 9
Interview by Fr. Antonio Spadaro, Editor-in-Chief of the Italian
Jesuit Magazine *La Civiltà Cattolica*. Rome. August 19, 23,
and 29, 2013.

October 10
General Audience. St. Peter's Square. May 22, 2013.

October 11
Address for the Closing of the Fourth World Congress Sponsored
by *Scholas Occurrentes*. Synod Hall. February 5, 2015.

October 12
Twitter post (Pontifex). June 6, 2014, 3:00 a.m.

October 13
Homily at Holy Mass for *Evangelium Vitae* Day. St. Peter's Square.
June 16, 2013.

October 14
General Audience. St. Peter's Square. June 5, 2013.

October 15
Message for World Mission Day 2014. Given June 8, 2014.

October 16
General Audience. St. Peter's Square. June 5, 2013.

October 17
Address to the Students of the Jesuit Schools of Italy and Albania.
Paul VI Audience Hall. June 7, 2013.

October 18

Interview by Fr. Antonio Spadaro, Editor-in-Chief of the Italian Jesuit Magazine *La Civiltà Cattolica*. Rome. August 19, 23, and 29, 2013.

October 19

Address on Vigil of Pentecost to Ecclesial Movements. St. Peter's Square. May 18, 2013.

October 20

Address to Members of the Diplomatic Corps Accredited to the Holy See. Sala Regia. January 13, 2014.

October 21

Address on Vigil of Pentecost to Ecclesial Movements. St. Peter's Square. May 18, 2013.

October 22

Homily at Holy Mass with Seminarians, Novices, and Those Discerning Their Vocation. Vatican Basilica. July 7, 2013.

October 23

General Audience. St. Peter's Square. June 5, 2013.

October 24

Apostolic Exhortation *The Joy of the Gospel* (*Evangelii Gaudium*), no. 213. November 24, 2013.

October 25

Apostolic Exhortation *The Joy of the Gospel* (*Evangelii Gaudium*), no. 53. November 24, 2013.

October 26
Message on the Occasion of the Twentieth Conference of the Parties to the United Nations Framework Convention on Climate Change (Lima, December 1-12, 2014). Given November 17, 2014.

October 27
Homily at Midnight Mas, Solemnity of the Nativity of the Lord. Vatican Basilica. December 24, 2014.

October 28
Address During Video Conference with Students of the *Scholas* Social Network. Synod Hall. September 4, 2014.

October 29
Interview by Fr. Antonio Spadaro, Editor-in-Chief of the Italian Jesuit Magazine *La Civiltà Cattolica*. Rome. August 19, 23, and 29, 2013.

October 30
Address to a Delegation from the *Dignitatis Humanae* Institute. Clementine Hall. December 7, 2013.

October 31
Homily at *Missa Pro Ecclesia* with the Cardinal Electors. Sistine Chapel. March 14, 2013.

NOVEMBER

November 1
Homily on the Solemnity of All Saints. Cemetery of Verano. November 1, 2013.

November 2
Homily on the Solemnity of All Saints. Cemetery of Verano. November 1, 2013.

November 3
Morning Meditation in the Chapel of the *Domus Sanctae Marthae*.
September 16, 2013.

November 4
Morning Meditation in the Chapel of the *Domus Sanctae Marthae*.
September 16, 2013.

November 5
Apostolic Exhortation *The Joy of the Gospel* (*Evangelii Gaudium*),
no. 205. November 24, 2013.

November 6
Apostolic Exhortation *The Joy of the Gospel* (*Evangelii Gaudium*),
no. 205. November 24, 2013.

November 7
Morning Meditation. Chapel of the *Domus Sanctae Marthae*.
September 25, 2014.

November 8
Homily on the Solemnity of All Saints. Cemetery of Verano.
November 1, 2013.

November 9
Morning Meditation. Chapel of the *Domus Sanctae Marthae*.
September 16, 2013. Vatican Radio translation.

November 10
Speech on the Occasion of the Twenty-Eighth World Youth Day.
Prayer Vigil with Young People, Waterfront of Copacabana, Rio de
Janeiro. July 27, 2013.

November 11

Message for the Seventieth Anniversary of the Normandy Landings. June 6, 2014. Catholic News Service translation.

November 12

Morning Meditation. Chapel of the *Domus Sanctae Marthae*. June 2, 2013.

November 13

Address to the New Non-Resident Ambassadors to the Holy See. Clementine Hall. May 16, 2013.

November 14

Morning Meditation. Chapel of the *Domus Sanctae Marthae*. May 22, 2013. Vatican Radio translation.

November 15

Address at Meeting with the Poor Assisted by Caritas. Assisi. October 4, 2013.

November 16

Address to the New Non-Resident Ambassadors to the Holy See. Clementine Hall. May 16, 2013.

November 17

Angelus. St. Peter's Square. February 9, 2014.

November 18

Address at Meeting with Families on Apostolic Journey to Sri Lanka and the Philippines (January 12-19, 2015). Mall of Asia Arena, Manila. January 16, 2015.

November 19
Interview by Fr. Antonio Spadaro, Editor-in-Chief of the Italian Jesuit Magazine *La Civiltà Cattolica*. Rome. August 19, 23, and 29, 2013.

November 20
General Audience. St. Peter's Square. February 11, 2014.

November 21
Homily at Holy Mass for the Marian Day on the Occasion of the Year of Faith. St. Peter's Square. October 1, 2013.

November 22
Angelus. St. Peter's Square. September 8, 2013.

November 23
Homily at Holy Mass for the Marian Day on the Occasion of the Year of Faith. St. Peter's Square. October 1, 2013.

November 24
Twitter post (Pontifex). March 20, 2014, 5:20 a.m.

November 25
Homily at Holy Chrism Mass on Holy Thursday. Vatican Basilica. April 17, 2014.

November 26
General Audience. St. Peter's Square. October 29, 2014.

November 27
Twitter post (Pontifex). January 18, 2015, 3:00 a.m.

November 28

General Audience. St. Peter's Square. March 4, 2015.

November 29

Address to the Members of the Diplomatic Corps Accredited to the Holy See. Sala Regia. January 12, 2015.

November 30

Apostolic Exhortation *The Joy of the Gospel* (*Evangelii Gaudium*), no. 7. November 24, 2013.

DECEMBER

December 1

Angelus. St. Peter's Square. December 1, 2013.

December 2

Address at Meeting with the Bishops of the United States on Apostolic Journey to Cuba and the United States of America (September 19-28). Cathedral of St. Matthew, Washington, DC. September 23, 2015.

December 3

General Audience. St. Peter's Square. February 18, 2015.

December 4

Interview by Fr. Antonio Spadaro, Editor-in-Chief of the Italian Jesuit Magazine *La Civiltà Cattolica*. Rome. August 19, 23, and 29, 2013.

December 5

Homily at Midnight Mass, Solemnity of the Nativity of the Lord. Vatican Basilica. December 24, 2013.

December 6
Regina Caeli During Pilgrimage to the Holy Land. Bethlehem. May 25, 2014.

December 7
Address at Prayer Vigil for the Festival of Families on Apostolic Journey to Cuba and the United States of America (September 19-28). B. Franklin Parkway, Philadelphia. September 26, 2015.

December 8
Angelus. St. Peter's Square. December 8, 2013.

December 9
Address to the National Numerous Family Association. Paul VI Audience Hall. December 28, 2014.

December 10
Homily at Midnight Mass, Solemnity of the Nativity of the Lord. Vatican Basilica. December 24, 2013.

December 11
Morning Meditation. Chapel of the *Domus Sanctae Marthae*. January 27, 2015.

December 12
Homily at Mass on the Feast of Our Lady of Guadalupe. Vatican Basilica. December 12, 2014.

December 13
Angelus. St. Peter's Square. January 4, 2015.

December 14
Twitter post (Pontifex). January 1, 2015, 12:30 a.m.

December 15
Twitter post (Pontifex). March 10, 2015, 2:00 a.m.

December 16
Angelus. St. Peter's Square. December 1, 2013.

December 17
Homily on Pastoral Visit to the Roman Parish San Giuseppe All'Aurelio. December 14, 2014.

December 18
Angelus. St. Peter's Square. December 7, 2014.

December 19
Homily at Holy Mass on the Occasion of the Twenty-Eighth World Youth Day. Basilica of the Shrine of Our Lady of the Conception of Aparecida. July 24, 2013.

December 20
Morning Meditation. Chapel of the *Domus Sanctae Marthae*. December 23, 2013.

December 21
Homily at Midnight Mass, Solemnity of the Nativity of the Lord. Vatican Basilica. December 24, 2013.

December 22
Address at Meeting with Personnel of the Holy See and Vatican City State. Paul VI Audience Hall. December 22, 2014.

December 23
Angelus. St. Peter's Square. December 15, 2013.

December 24
Homily at Midnight Mass, Solemnity of the Nativity of the Lord. Vatican Basilica. December 24, 2014.

December 25
Urbi et Orbi Message. Christmas 2014. Given December 25, 2014.

December 26
Homily at Midnight Mass, Solemnity of the Nativity of the Lord. Vatican Basilica. December 24, 2014.

December 27
Twitter post (Pontifex). June 18, 2015, 11:40 a.m.

December 28
Urbi et Orbi Message. Christmas 2014. Given December 25, 2014.

December 29
Urbi et Orbi Message. Christmas 2014. Given December 25, 2014.

December 30
Urbi et Orbi Message. Christmas 2013. Given December 25, 2013.

December 31
Twitter post (Pontifex). January 23, 2014, 2:23 a.m.